Careers
in Focus

Retail

Ferguson Publishing Company
Chicago, Illinois

Andrew Morkes, *Managing Editor-Career Publications*
Carol Yehling, *Senior Editor*
Anne Paterson, *Editor*
Nora Walsh, *Editorial Assistant*

Copyright © 2001 Ferguson Publishing Company
ISBN 0-89434-357-2

Library of Congress Cataloging-in-Publication Data

Careers in Focus: Retail
    p. cm.
    Includes index.
    ISBN 0-89434-357-2
        1. Retail trade--Vocational guidance. 2. Selling--Vocational guidance.
3. Sales personnel--Job descriptions. [1. Retail trade--Vocational guidance.
2. Selling--Vocational guidance. 3. Sales personnel. 4. Vocational guidance.]
I. Title: Retail. II. Ferguson Publishing Company

HF5429.29 .C37 2000
381'.1'02373--dc21

                                                                00-039388

Printed in the United States of America

Cover photo courtesy Steven Peters/Tony Stone Images

Published and distributed by
Ferguson Publishing Company
200 West Jackson Boulevard, 7th Floor
Chicago, Illinois 60606
800-306-9941
www.fergpubco.com

X-8

Table of Contents

Introduction

Although shopping in a retail store, from a catalog, or from the Internet is a common activity, the actual work of a retail organization is a mystery to most people. One of the primary tasks of retail stores is to be constantly aware of the changing lifestyle habits, needs, and desires of its customers. They must anticipate the customers' wishes days, weeks, and even months ahead of time. In addition, because of their competition, retailers must race to get the merchandise first, to offer the best service, and to provide the most attractive setting so that customers will be lured into their particular establishment.

In general, stores can be divided into two major groups: specialty stores and general merchandise stores. *Specialty stores* carry just one category of merchandise or several types of closely related merchandise. Specialty stores include apparel shops, building supply stores, automobile dealers, gas stations, household appliance stores, florists, optical goods stores, news stands, drugstores, shoe stores, sporting goods stores, computer sales outlets, grocery stores, and supermarkets.

General merchandise stores include variety stores, junior department stores, and department stores. They stock a multitude of different items under one roof. Variety stores carry broad assortments of goods at limited prices. Junior department stores carry various categories of merchandise in somewhat broader price ranges. Department stores carry large assortments of apparel, home goods, and staple items in even more extensive price ranges. When specialty stores or general merchandise stores feature self-service and bargain prices, they usually are called mass merchandisers.

Some stores have only a single location, while others, such as chain organizations and franchise operations, have more than one. The largest stores have several thousand locations. Chain organizations are parent stores with branches. Franchise operations allow individually owned stores to market or sell their line of goods.

The major functions of retailing may be divided into five categories: merchandising and buying, store operations, sales promotion, bookkeeping/accounting, and personnel. Merchandising and buying determines the assortment and amount of merchandise to be sold. Store operations maintains the retailer's building. Sales promotion and advertising inform customers and potential customers about the goods and services that are available. Bookkeeping and accounting workers are charged with the task of keeping records of money spent and received, as well as records of payrolls, taxes, and money due from customers. The personnel department staffs the store with qualified people.

Many people are involved in buying merchandise in large organizations, whereas in small stores one or two persons may do all the buying. Before merchandise can be purchased, however, store executives must plan for the kinds and amounts of merchandise to be bought. Analyses of previous sales reveal how successful the store was in selling similar merchandise during a comparable period. After these records are examined and the amount of such merchandise already in the store is determined, an executive decides on the amount of new merchandise to be purchased. The person who does this kind of planning and supervising in a large organization may be called a merchandiser or merchandise manager.

After the general buying plan has been established, the buyer must go to manufacturers' showrooms or to factories in the United States or abroad to look at the merchandise and select from the available items that will be in demand for the coming season. Contracts then are signed for the delivery of the goods. Buying may be completed as much as six months before the buyer anticipates selling the goods in the store.

Store managers of chain stores and department managers in branch stores are responsible not only for merchandise but also for department or store operation. The department manager acts as a departmental supervisor for the buyer in the branch store but does not have the responsibility for actual selection and purchase of merchandise.

In a small store, usually one store manager has final responsibility for all operational activities. In a larger organization each function may be supervised by a separate manager. Managers could be in charge of receiving goods, marking them, placing them in the stockrooms or warehouse, and subsequently moving the goods to the selling floor. After the merchandise is sold, other managers may be in charge of wrapping stations and delivery services. Supervision of the selling floor and handling of customer returns and complaints also are activities carried out by operating personnel. Elevator service, housekeeping service, and the relocation of goods for special selling seasons are further responsibilities of operating personnel.

Many large retail organizations maintain sales promotion, advertising, and display staffs. The people who work in these fields are responsible for the overall impression that the store creates. A favorable image generates more business for the retailer. Those who produce advertising include the advertising manager, copywriters, artists, photographers, and typographers.

Most of the positions in marketing require creative talent. Therefore, those who apply for these jobs usually excel in writing or artwork, or they have had experience in staging shows or running school publicity events.

In small stores, most owners or managers employ part-time accountants to take care of the financial records of the firm. The finances of a large store or chain of stores usually are administered by a controller, who has an accounting background and knowledge of computer systems.

Retailing in today's economy demands both knowledge of the field and management ability. More competition, better educated customers, and more diversified types of retailing allow for fewer errors, especially on the part of small firm owners. Also a challenge for U.S. retailers is the country's maturing population, its rapidly changing culture, an influx of people from other countries, and a growth in technology, all of which provide a more dynamic and less predictable market. Because retailing is still primarily a business of people working with and serving other people, the use of computerized systems for record keeping, merchandise-handling mechanization, and automatic vending machines has not displaced many sales workers.

The Internet is now changing the way that mass retailers do business and it will continue to have a huge impact in the future. According to the International Mass Retailers Association, sales over the Internet are expected to reach between $10 and $16 billion by 2000. The benefit of selling on the Internet for retailers is the ability to reach new customers, both domestic and foreign, and at a much lower cost. Consumers have the convenience of shopping from home or office for groceries, clothes, or insurance, as well as planning a vacation.

Each article in this book discusses a particular retail industry occupation in detail. The information comes from Ferguson's *Encyclopedia of Careers and Vocational Guidance*. The **History** section describes the history of the particular job as it relates to the overall development of its industry or field. The **Job** describes the primary and secondary duties of the job. **Requirements** discusses high school and postsecondary education and training requirements, any certification or licensing necessary, and any other personal requirements for success in the job. **Exploring** offers suggestions on how to gain some experience in or knowledge of the particular job before making a firm educational and financial commitment. The focus is on what can be done while still in high school (or in the early years of college) to gain a better understanding of the job. The **Employers** section gives an overview of typical places of employment for the job. **Starting Out** discusses the best ways to land that first job, be it through the college placement office, newspaper ads, or personal contact. The **Advancement** section describes what kind of career path to expect from the job and how to get there. **Earnings** lists salary ranges and describes the typical fringe benefits. The **Work Environment** section describes the typical surroundings and conditions of employment—whether indoors or outdoors, noisy or quiet, social or independent, and so on. Also discussed are typical hours worked, any seasonal fluctuations, and the stresses and strains of the job. The **Outlook** section summarizes the job in terms of the general economy and industry projections. For the most part, Outlook information is obtained from the Bureau of Labor Statistics and is supplemented by information taken from professional associations. Job growth terms follow those used in the *Occupational Outlook Handbook*: Growth described as "much faster than the average" means an increase of 36 percent or more. Growth described as "faster than the average" means an increase of 21 to 35 percent. Growth described as "about as fast as the average" means an increase of 10 to 20 percent. Growth described as "little change or more slowly than the average" means an increase of 0 to 9 percent. "Decline" means a decrease of 1 percent or more.

Each article ends with **For More Information**, which lists organizations that can provide career information on training, education, internships, scholarships, and job placement.

Antique Dealers

Overview

An antique is an object that is highly valued as a work of art or as a relic of a particular time period. By strict definition, antiques can be defined as items more than 100 years old. However, over the last two decades, the term antique has been applied to furniture, jewelry, clothing, art, household goods, and many other collectibles, dating back to as recently as the 1970s. People that make a living acquiring, displaying, and selling antiques are called *antique dealers*. Many antique dealers are self-employed. The Antiques & Collectibles Dealers Association estimates there are approximately 200,000 to 250,000 antique dealers in the United States, based in antique shops, antique malls, and on the Internet.

History

Interest in antiques can be traced back to the Renaissance when people began to admire and prize Greek and Roman antiquities such as coins, manuscripts, sculptures, art, and pieces of architecture. In order to fulfill public interest and curiosity, as well as to supply the growing number of private and public collections, many antiquities from Egypt, Italy, and Greece were looted and carried off to other countries. The antique market, as it is known today, consists of everyday household objects, as well as furniture, clothing, art, and even automobiles, originating from another time period. After World War I, interest in antiques grew; many people began to collect, preserve, and display pieces in their homes. As interest grew, so did the need for antique businesses and dealers.

There are different categories of antiques, and different ways and reasons to collect them. Some people choose to collect pieces from different time periods such as American Colonial or Victorian; others collect by the pattern or brand—Chippendale furniture or Coca-Cola memorabilia are some examples. Some people collect objects related to their career or business. For example, a physician may collect early surgical instruments, or a pharmacist, antique apothecary cabinets. A growing category in the antiques industry is ephemera. Ephemera includes theater programs, postcards, cigarette cards, and food labels, among others. These items were produced without lasting value or survival in mind. Though many pieces of ephemera can be purchased inexpensively, others, especially if they are among the first of their kind, or in excellent condition, are rare and considered very valuable.

Some larger antique dealers specialize and deal only with items from a particular time period, or design. Most, however, are considered General Line antique dealers, meaning they collect, buy, and sell most previously owned household items. Such shops will carry antiques ranging from dining room furniture to jewelry to cooking molds.

The idea of what is antique and worth collecting constantly changes with time and the public's tastes and interests. Items representing the rock music industry of the 1960s and 1970s, as well as household items and furniture of the 1970s, are highly sought after today. Antique dealers not only stock their stores with items currently in demand, but keep an eye on the collectibles of the future.

The Job

For Sandra Naujokas, proprietor of Favorite Things Antique Shop, in Orland Park, Illinois, the antiques business is never boring. Twenty-five years ago, she started a collection of English-style china, and she's been hooked on antiques and collecting ever since. Naujokas spends her work day greeting customers and answering any questions they may have. When business slows down, she cleans the store and prices inventory. Sometimes people will bring in items for resale; it's up to Naujokas to carefully inspect each piece and settle on a price. She relies on pricing manuals such as *Kovel's Guide* and *Schroeder's Insider & Price Update*, which give guidelines and a suggested price on a wide range of items.

Naujokas also goes on a number of shopping expeditions a year to restock her store. Besides rummage sales and auctions, she relies on buying trips to different parts of the country and abroad to find regional items. At times, she is invited to a person's home to view items for sale. "It's important to be open to all possibilities," Naujokas says.

She also participates in several shows a year, in order to reach customers that normally would not travel to the store's location. "You need to do a variety of things to advertise your wares," Naujokas advises. She also promotes her business by advertising in her town's travel brochure, the local newspapers, and by direct mail campaigns. Her schedule is grueling, as the store is open seven days a week, but Naujokas enjoys the work and the challenge of being an antique dealer. Besides the social aspect of antiquing, and interacting with all sorts of people and situations, she loves having the first choice of items for her personal collections. Her advice for people interested in having their own antique store? "You have to really like the items you intend to sell."

Requirements

High School

You can become an antique dealer with a high school diploma, though many successful antique dealers have become specialists in their field partly through further education. While in high school, concentrate on history classes, as well as art, to familiarize yourself with the particular significance and details of different periods in time and art. Also, consider studying home economics if you plan to specialize in household items; it will help to know the difference between a wooden rolling pin and wooden butter paddle.

Advanced classes in communications will also be helpful. This is a people-oriented business—it pays to be able to deal efficiently with different types of people and situations. Operating your own small business will also require skills such as accounting, simple bookkeeping, and marketing.

Postsecondary Training

While a college education is not required, a degree in art or history will give you a working knowledge of the antiques you sell and the historical periods they originated in. A degree in business or entrepreneurship will give you the training that will help you to run a successful business.

Certification or Licensing

Presently, there are no certification programs available for antique dealers. However, if you wish to conduct appraisals, it will be necessary to take the proper appraisal course—depending on your interest or antique specialty—and obtain certification. Also, if you plan to open your own antique store, then you will need a business license.

Other Requirements

You'll need patience—and lots of it. Keeping your store well stocked with antiques and other collectibles takes numerous buying trips to auctions, estate sales, flea markets, rummage sales, and even abroad. Many times you'll have to sort through boxes of ordinary "stuff" before coming across a treasure. Worse yet, unless you're lucky enough to have a large staff, you will have to make these outings by yourself. Tact is another must-have quality for success in this industry. Remember the old adage—one person's trash is another person's treasure.

Exploring

If you want to explore this field further, you may want to start by visiting an antique store. If you see valuable treasures as opposed to old furniture, outdated books, or dusty collectibles, then chances are this is the job for you.

You can also tune to an episode of public television's traveling antique show, "The Antique Road Show." The premise? Locals are encouraged to bring family treasures or rummage sale bargains for appraisal by antique industry experts.

Employers

Many antique dealers are self-employed, operating their own shops or renting space at a local antique mall. Others work as employees of larger antique dealers.

Starting Out

All dealers have a great interest in antiques and are collectors themselves. Oftentimes, their businesses result from an overabundance of their personal collections. There are many ways to build your collection and create inventory worthy of an antique business. Attending yard sales is an inexpensive way to build your inventory; you'll never know what kind of valuables you will come across. Flea markets and antique malls will provide great purchasing opportunities, as well as a good chance to check out the competition. Naujokas finds the spring an especially busy time; it seems many people decide, while doing seasonal cleaning, to part with many household items they no longer need.

Advancement

For those renting showcase space at antique malls or larger antique shops, or working from their homes, advancement in this field can mean opening your own antique store. Your new store is more than an extension of your hobby—it's your business and livelihood, so treat it as such. Besides a business license, you'll need to apply for a seller's permit and a state tax identification number. Check with your local government for details since requirements vary by state.

You will also want to devise a system of inventory to keep track of the items in your store. Consider some ways of advertising and marketing to keep your business in the public's eye. If you need help or have any questions, the library, bookstore, or the Internet can offer information regarding the basics of opening and running your own business. Don't forget to turn to people who are already in the antique business. They may be able to offer the best advice of all.

Earnings

It is difficult to gauge what antique dealers earn because of the vastness of the industry. Some internationally known, high-end antique stores dealing with many pieces of priceless furniture or works of art may make million of dollars in yearly profits. This, however, is the exception; it is impossible, and quite unfair to compare the high end dealer with the lower end market. The majority of antique dealers are comparatively small in size and type of inventory; some dealers work only part-time, or rent showcase space from established antique shops. According to a recent survey conducted by the Antiques & Collectibles Dealer Association, the average antique showcase dealer earns about $1,000 a month in gross profits. From there, each dealer earns a net profit as determined by the piece or pieces sold, minus overhead and other business costs. Note that annual earnings vary greatly for antique dealers due to factors such as size and specialization of the store, location, the market, and current trends and tastes of the public.

Work Environment

Much of your time will be spent indoors. Many antique stores do not operate with a large staff, so be prepared, many times, to work alone. Also, there may be large gaps of time between customers. Most stores are open at least five days a week and operate during regular business hours, though some have extended shopping hours in the evening.

Don't worry, you won't be indoors all the time. Buying trips and shopping expeditions will give you opportunities for travel as well as shopping to restock your inventory. Naujokas finds the spring the busiest time for buying and selecting her store's merchandise, while the holiday season is a busy selling time.

Outlook

According to the Antiques & Collectibles Dealers Association (ACDA), the antiques industry should enjoy moderate growth in future years. The Internet has quickly become a popular way to buy and sell antiques. Though this medium has introduced antique collecting to many people worldwide, it has also had an adverse affect on the industry, namely for dealers and businesses that sell antiques in more traditional settings such as a shop, mall, or at an antique show. However, Jim Tucker, founder and director of the ACDA, predicts that the popularity of Web sites devoted to selling antiques will level off. There is a great social aspect to antiquing; people want to see, feel, and touch the items they are interested in purchasing.

Though the number of traditional antiques—items more than 100 years old—is limited, new items will be in vogue as collectibles. Also, people will be ready to sell old furniture and other belongings to make room for new, modern purchases. It is unlikely that there will ever be a shortage of inventory worthy of an antique shop.

For More Information

For industry information, antique show schedules, appraisal information, or a copy of The World of Antiques & Collectibles, *contact:*

Antiques & Collectibles Dealers Associations
PO Box 2782
Huntersville, NC 28070
Tel: 800-287-7127
Email: acda-info@acda.org
Web: http://www.acda.org

For information about appraisals or appraising, contact:

International Society of Appraisers
16040 Christensen Road, Suite 102
Seattle, WA 98188-2965
Tel: 206-241-0359
Web: http://www.isa-appraisers.org

Auctioneers

Overview

Auctioneers appraise, assemble, and advertise goods, which they subsequently sell to the highest bidder during an auction. They act as salespeople for the family, company, or agency selling the items to be auctioned. Depending on their area of expertise, they may auction off anything from a rare book to an entire office building.

History

In the United States many of the oldest auction firms are located in cities on the East Coast. Auctions, though, have long been popular in rural areas. Prior to the development of department stores, rural families had their own methods of dispensing with and acquiring the items and machinery they needed. For small or individual items, a barter or trade sometimes was made to exchange a needed tool or other possession. When many different items were being sold, however, a family would hold an auction, and an auctioneer would be hired to assist the family in disposing of the property. Families sometimes held auctions to raise cash or because they were moving and could not take along all their possessions.

Auctions are a popular way to buy farm equipment, real estate, artwork, livestock, or personal property from estates. An auction disposes of many varied items fairly quickly by selling one item to the highest bidder and then immediately moving through the rest of the collection. Auctions also are a popular way to raise money for charities and other groups. They are fun as well as functional and have become increasingly common in both rural areas and cities.

The Job

An auctioneer's work has two main facets: the preliminary preparation and evaluation and the selling itself. The former takes more time and skill and is less familiar to most people. Prior to the auction itself, the auctioneer meets with the sellers to review the property to be sold. The auctioneer makes note of the lowest bid, called the "reserved bid," that the sellers will accept for each item. The auctioneer also advises clients when an item should be sold "absolute," or without a minimum bid. If there are legal issues to be discussed, an auctioneer confers with the sellers.

The most time-consuming activity often is the appraisal of the goods. The auctioneer determines the value of each item and compares it to the reserve bid established by the sellers. The auctioneer makes notes on the type of item being sold, its history, and any unique qualities the item may have. This background information can encourage higher bids and increase buyer interest.

Once the appraisal has taken place, an auctioneer must organize the items in the area where the auction is to be held. Sometimes the auctioneer issues a catalog or booklet describing the items for sale for that particular day. The catalog also may list the sequence in which the items will be sold so buyers know when the items they want will be up for sale. In addition to the catalog, auctioneers organize any advertising needed to promote the sale. Newspaper and magazine ads, flyers, signs, and broadcast announcements can reach people from many different areas and bring in a large crowd. Some rural areas hold auctions as special attractions for tourists around summer holidays or to commemorate town events and local celebrations.

Usually the auctioneer organizes and sets up the auction far enough in advance for people to come early, peruse the area, and see what is of interest to them. Antique furniture and clothing, farm equipment, and artwork are some of the things sold at auctions. Other auctions concentrate on large industrial machinery or cars, as well as livestock, stamps, coins, and books.

The auctioneer works to help both the buyer and the seller. An auctioneer is familiar enough with the potential value of the items to begin bids at a certain price. The encouragement and stimulation an auctioneer provides, however, often is matched by the excitement and competition among the buyers. Auctioneers must be quick-thinking and comfortable addressing crowds, not only offering them information about the items for sale but at times acting as entertainers to keep the crowd interested.

Auctioneers coordinate the pace of the auction and judge which items should be sold first. Sometimes to boost people's interest, an auctioneer saves the most popular items for last. At other times the best articles are sold first so that those who weren't able to purchase their first choice will feel free to bid on other items.

Auctioneers commonly enlist the help of assistants, who carry items to the auctioneer, ensuring a steady flow of goods. In addition, another assistant may be in charge of collecting money, issuing receipts, and keeping track of the purchaser of each item. Most auctions follow a typical pattern. The items for sale are made available for inspection in a catalog or a display. In the case of real estate auctions, however, photographs may be circulated. In some instances, land that is miles away can be sold, though the auctioneer will describe some history and features of the area. Often these types of auctions take less time, but the preparation is more detailed. Auctioneers must know the dimensions of the buildings they are selling, boundary lines for lots and farms, and whether any money is owed or any environmental hazard exists on the property, as well as information about the terms of payment and zoning laws.

Requirements

High School

A high school diploma generally is a basic requirement for auctioneers. Classes in sales, mathematics, speech, art, art history, and economics are useful.

Postsecondary Training

Training for auctioneers is available at many schools, such as the Missouri Auction School in Kansas City. More advanced training is provided by the National Auctioneers Association (NAA), which holds classes in numerous locations around the country. The Auction Marketing Institute (AMI), an organization affiliated with the NAA, offers the Certified Auctioneers Institute profession program, taught at Indiana University in Bloomington. One can also receive training in the Accredited Auctioneer Real Estate program, also sponsored by the AMI; classes for this program are held in various places in the United States.

Auctioneer training can involve appraising and item presentation, as well as speech classes so that auctioneers do not strain their voices while working long hours. Auctioneers who plan to concentrate on specific areas may take classes to supplement their training. Livestock and real estate auctions require specialized knowledge. In addition, some auctioneers have backgrounds in art or antiques.

Auctioneers must be effective speakers. Their job is to command attention and interest in the items through the power of their voice and their personal manner and good humor. Auctioneers should have a great deal of stamina, since auctions often take place outdoors in warm weather and can last for many hours at a stretch. Auctioneers must also be alert so they can keep track of the crowd activity, the progress of the assistants, and the selling of the goods.

Because of all the deliberation that goes into preparing an auction, an auctioneer should like working with people. A keen sense of evaluation and an honest nature also are useful attributes.

Certification or Licensing

Because they handle large sums of money, most auctioneers are bonded; however, licensing for auctioneers varies from state to state. Some auctioneers are required to pass examinations and pay licensing fees. A professional designation, Certified Auctioneers Institute (CAI) is awarded to practicing auctioneers who meet the experiential, educational, and ethical standards set by the Auction Marketing Institute.

Other Requirements

Auctioneers who work in specialized areas, such as real estate and livestock, must conform to additional regulations. Those who sell land must be licensed real estate sales agents or brokers. Auctioneers should be familiar with laws and regulations in the states in which they practice.

Exploring

High school students wishing to explore the field should attend some auctions and see firsthand the responsibilities that are involved. Classes in speech, drama, and communications may be helpful because auctioneers rely heavily on their voices, not only for speaking and presentation but also to get the buyer's attention through style and performance.

More direct involvement is possible as well. Charities and other social organizations occasionally use nonprofessionals for fund-raising auctions, and established auctioneers often hire part-time assistants. It may also be useful to read periodicals, such as *Auctioneer* (published by the National Auctioneers Association), that publish articles about the field.

Employers

Auctioneers often work as consultants on a freelance basis. They may be hired by private individuals or large companies anywhere that goods are offered for sale to the highest bidder. Others may work for private auction houses, which usually are located in large metropolitan areas such as New York, Los Angeles, and Chicago, as well as smaller cities. Those who wish to focus on specific areas such as real estate, art, or farm equipment should, of course, seek consulting assignments or permanent positions in locations and/or with companies where these items are sold; for example, farm equipment generally is auctioned in rural areas.

Starting Out

Beginning auctioneers may work as assistants, handling money and receipts or presenting the sale items to the experienced auctioneer. They also may begin by working local and county fairs or smaller auctions.

Professional trade schools may offer placement services or internships that link beginners with established practitioners. Beginners may have to work part-time until they gain experience and become better known. Auctioneers who work for large auction houses may receive more assignments as they become more experienced and complete training offered by the firm.

Advancement

Professional auctioneers must have a reputation for skilled and honest performance. Since most auctioneers get paid by commission, they may decide to specialize in selling real estate, farm equipment, or artwork—areas that are likely to bring in more revenue for less preparation and shorter presentations.

Auctioneers who work with auction houses may move up the ranks and obtain more prestigious assignments. Auctioneers also advance as they develop their knowledge in specialized areas. Some people move into different lines of work but keep auctioning as a side job.

Earnings

Auctioneers have the potential to earn above-average wages. In the late 1990s part-time auctioneers earned close to $10,000, while full-time auctioneers typically earned more than $20,000. The best-paid auctioneers earned $50,000 to $100,000 or more. On a daily basis, pay ranges between $100 and $2,000.

Auctioneers usually are paid on commission. Part-time auctioneers sometimes supplement their income by assisting more experienced workers, acting as cashiers, assisting with publicity, or helping to organize the items.

Work Environment

Because auctioneers often travel to an assignment, they may encounter a wide range of working conditions. Auctions are held year round. They take place in cities and small towns and occur in all types of weather. Auctioneers may work inside in a large hall or outside during a state fair. The type of goods being sold may also dictate their working conditions; for instance, farm equipment is commonly sold outdoors on the site of the owner's farm.

Auctioneers often are provided with a podium and a microphone, which are especially important at large auctions, which can draw more than 2,000 people. This allows the auctioneer to keep the crowd's attention when the noise and activity level become distracting or stressful.

Outlook

The outlook for auctioneers is good, especially for those who have developed a specialty, such as real estate. Auctioneers with polished skills and a strong delivery usually have little trouble finding work. For an ambitious auctioneer who is willing to travel to various locations and invest time to gain experience, regular employment is possible, either as an independent auctioneer or as a staff member of an auction firm.

Many auctioneers get assignments based on their reputation and notoriety within an area. Thus, auctioneers may find it difficult to reestablish themselves if they move to another area. Also, some types of auctions are found only in certain areas. Art auctions, for example, generally take place in cities, while livestock, farm equipment, and farm land most often are sold in rural areas.

For More Information

Contact the following organization for a school packet, or for a copy of the brochure, The Auction Professional.

National Auctioneers Association
8880 Ballentine
Overland Park, KS 66214-1985
Attn: Director of Membership
Tel: 913-541-8084
Web: http://www.auctioneers.org

For information on continuing education and certification for auctioneers already in the industry, contact:

Auction Marketing Institute Inc.
8880 Ballentine
Overland Park, KS 66214
Tel: 913-541-8115
Web: http://www.auctionmarketing.org/

For information about the school, contact:

Florida Auctioneer Academy
10376 East Colonial Drive
Orlando, FL 32817
Tel: 800-422-9155
Web: http://www.f-a-a.com/

For an information packet and cassette tape about the school, send a note marked "Careers" to:

Missouri Auction School
Distribution Center
#10 Lanco Drive
Morrilton, AR 72110
Tel: 800-835-1955

School address:
213 South 5th Street
St. Joseph, MO 64501

Automobile Sales Workers

Business Speech	School Subjects
Communication/ideas Helping/teaching	Personal Skills
Primarily indoors Primarily one location	Work Environment
High school diploma	Minimum Education Level
$20,000 to $35,360 to $50,000+	Salary Range
Voluntary	Certification or Licensing
About as fast as the average	Outlook

Overview

Automobile sales workers inform customers about new or used automobiles, and they prepare payment, financing, and insurance papers for customers who have purchased a vehicle. It is their job to persuade the customer that the product they are selling is the best choice. They prospect new customers by mail, telephone, or through personal contacts. To stay informed about their products, sales workers regularly attend training sessions about the vehicles they sell.

History

By the 1920s, nearly 20,000 automobile dealerships dotted the American landscape as the "Big Three" automobile makers—Ford, General Motors, and Chrysler—increased production every year to meet the public's growing demand for automobiles. Automobile sales workers began to earn higher and higher wages. As automobiles became more popular, the need for an organization to represent the growing industry became evident. In 1917, the National Automobile Dealers Association was founded to change the way Congress viewed automobiles. In the early years, NADA worked to convince Congress that cars weren't luxuries, as they had been classified, but vital to the economy. The group prevented the government from converting all automotive factories to wartime work during World War I and reduced a proposed luxury tax on automobiles from 5 percent to 3 percent.

During the lean years of the Depression in the early 1930s, automobile sales fell sharply until President Franklin Delano Roosevelt's New Deal helped jumpstart the industry. Roosevelt signed the Code of Fair Competition for the Motor Vehicle Retailing Trade, which established standards in the automotive manufacturing and sales industries. By 1942, the number of dealerships in the United States more than doubled to 44,000.

Automobile sales workers have suffered an image problem for much of the career's history. Customers sometimes felt that they were pressured to purchase new cars at unfair prices and that the dealer's profit was too large. The 1958 Price Labeling Law, which mandated cars display window stickers listing manufacturer suggested retail prices and other information, helped ease relations between sales workers and their customers. However, in the fiercely competitive automobile market, sales workers' selling methods and the thrifty customer remained at odds.

When it came to used vehicles, there was no way for customers to know whether they were getting a fair deal. Even in the automobile's early history, used vehicles have been popular. From 1919 through the 1950s, used car sales consistently exceeded new car sales. Despite the popularity of used vehicles, the automobile sales industry didn't quite know how to handle them. Some dealers lost money on trade-ins when they stayed on the lot too long. After debating for years how to handle trade-ins, dealers finally began today's common practice of applying their value toward down payments on new cars.

The industry suffered personnel shortages when the armed forces recruited mechanics during World War II. This affected the service departments of dealerships, which traditionally have generated the biggest profits, and many dealers had to be creative to stay in business. During these lean times, sales gimmicks, such as giveaways and contests came into increased use. According to a history of NADA, one Indiana dealer bought radios, refrigerators, freezers, and furnaces to sell in his showroom and sold toys at Christmas to stay in business.

The energy crisis of the 1970s brought hard times to the entire automotive industry. Many dealerships were forced to close, and those that survived made little profit. In 1979 alone, 600 dealerships closed. Today there are

22,400 dealerships nationwide (down from 47,500 in 1951) accounting for 18 percent of all retail sales and employing more than 950,000 people. Most dealerships today sell more makes of cars than dealerships of the past. Still, they face competition from newer forms of automobile retailers, such as automotive superstores, the automotive equivalent to discount stores like Wal-Mart. Also, automotive information is becoming more widely available on the Internet, eroding the consumer's need for automobile sales workers as a source of information about automobiles.

The Job

The automobile sales worker's main task is to sell. Today, many dealerships try to soften the image of salesmen and women by emphasizing no pressure, even one-price shopping. But automobile dealers expect their employees to sell, and selling in most cases involves some degree of persuasion. The automobile sales worker informs customers of everything there is to know about a particular vehicle. A good sales worker finds out what the customer wants or needs and suggests automobiles that may fit that need—empowering the customer with choice and a feeling that he or she is getting a fair deal.

Since the sticker price on new cars is only a starting point to be bargained down, and since many customers come to dealerships already knowing which car they would like to buy, sales workers spend much of their time negotiating the final selling price.

Most dealerships have special sales forces for new cars, used cars, trucks, recreational vehicles, and leasing operations. In each specialty, sales workers learn all aspects of the product they must sell. They may attend information and training seminars sponsored by manufacturers. New car sales workers, especially, are constantly learning new car features. Sales workers inform customers about a car's performance, fuel economy, safety features, and luxuries or accessories. They are able to talk about innovations over previous models, engine and mechanical specifications, ease of handling, and ergonomic designs. Good sales workers also keep track of competing models' features.

In many ways, used car sales workers have a more daunting mass of information to keep track of. Whereas new car sales workers concentrate on the most current features of an automobile, used car sales workers must keep track of all features from several model years. Good used car dealers can look at a car and note immediately the make, model, and year of a car. Because of popular two- and three-year leasing options, the used car market has increased by nearly 50 percent in the last 10 years.

Successful sales workers are generally good readers of a person's character. They can determine exactly what it is a customer is looking for in a new car. They must be friendly and understanding of customers' needs in order to put them at ease (due to the amount of money involved, car buying is an unpleasant task for most people). They are careful not to oversell the car by providing the customers with information they may not care about or understand, thus confusing them. For example, if a customer only cares about style, sales workers will not impress upon him all of the wonderful intricacies of a new high-tech engine design.

Sales workers greet customers and ask if they have any questions about a particular model. It's very important for sales workers to have immediate and confident answers to all questions about the vehicles they're selling. When a sale is difficult, they occasionally use psychological methods, or subtle "prodding," to influence customers. Some sales workers use aggressive selling methods and pressure the customer to purchase the car. Although recent trends are turning away from the pressure-sell, competition will keep these types of selling methods prevalent in the industry, albeit at a slightly toned-down level.

Customers usually make more than one visit to a dealership before purchasing a new or used car. Because one sales worker "works" the customer on the first visit—forming an acquaintanceship and learning the customer's personality—he or she will usually stay with that customer until the sale is made or lost. The sales worker usually schedules times for the customer to come in and talk more about the car in order to stay with the customer through the process and not lose the sale to another sales worker. Sales workers may make follow-up phone calls to make special offers or remind customers of certain features that make a particular model better than the competition, or they may send mailings for the same purpose.

In addition to providing the customer with information about the car, sales workers discuss financing packages, leasing options, and warranty. When the sale is made, they go over the contract with the customer and obtain a signature. Frequently the exact model with all of the features the customer requested is not in the dealership, and the sales worker must place an order with the manufacturer or distributor. When purchasing a new or used vehicle many customers trade in their old vehicle. Sales workers appraise the trade-in and offer a price.

At some dealerships sales workers also do public relations and marketing work. They establish promotions to get customers into their showrooms, print fliers to distribute in the local community, and make television advertisements. In order to keep their name in the back (or front) of the customer's mind, they may send past customers birthday and holiday cards or similar "courtesies." Most of the larger dealerships also have an auto maintenance and repair service department. Sales workers may help customers establish a periodic maintenance schedule or suggest repair work.

Computers are used at a growing number of dealerships. Customers use computers to answer questions they may have, consult price indexes, check on ready availability of parts, and even compare the car they're interested in with the competition's equivalent. Although computers can't replace human interaction and sell the car to customers who need reassurances, they do help the customer feel more informed and more in control when buying a car.

Requirements

High School

Because thorough knowledge of automobiles—from how they work to how they drive and how they are manufactured—is essential for a successful sales worker, automotive maintenance classes in high school are an excellent place to begin. Classes in English, speech, drama, and psychology will help students achieve the excellent speaking skills they will need to make a good sale and gain customer confidence and respect. Classes in business and mathematics will teach students to manage and prioritize their work load, prepare goals, and work confidently with customer financing packages. As computers become increasingly prevalent in every aspect of the industry, students should take as many computer classes as they can. Students who can speak a second language are at an advantage, especially in major cities with large minority populations.

Postsecondary Training

Those who seek management-level positions will have a distinct advantage if they possess a college degree, preferably in business or marketing, but other degrees, whether they be in English, economics, or psychology, are no less important, so long as applicants have good management skills and can sell cars. Many schools offer degrees in automotive marketing and automotive aftermarket management which prepare students to take high-level management positions. Even with a two- or four-year degree in hand, many dealerships may not begin new hires directly as managers, but first start them out as a sales worker.

Certification or Licensing

By completing the Certified Automotive Merchandiser (CAM) program offered by the National Automobile Dealers Association, students seeking entry-level positions gain a significant advantage. Certification assures employers that workers have the basic skills they require.

Other Requirements

In today's competitive job market you will need a high school diploma to land a job that offers growth possibilities, a good salary, and challenges; this includes jobs in the automobile sales industry. Employers prefer to hire entry-level employees who have had some previous experience in automotive services or in retail sales. They look for candidates who have good verbal, business, mathematics, electronics, and computer skills. A number of automotive sales and services courses and degrees are offered today at community colleges, vocational schools, independent organizations, and manufacturers. Sales workers should possess a valid driver's license and have a good driving record.

Sales workers must be enthusiastic, well organized, self-starters who thrive in a competitive environment. They must show excitement and authority about each type of car they sell and convince customers, without being too pushy (though some pressure on the customer usually helps make the sale), that the car they're interested in is the "right" car, at the fairest price. Sales workers must be able to read a customer's personality and know when to be outgoing and when to pull back and be more reserved. A neat, professional appearance is also very important for sales workers.

Exploring

Automobile trade magazines and books, in addition to selling technique and business books, are excellent sources of information for someone considering a career in this field. Local and state automobile and truck dealer associations can also provide you with information on career possibilities in automobile and truck sales. Your local Yellow Pages has a listing under "associations" for dealer organizations in your area.

Students interested in automobile sales work might first stop by their local dealer and ask about training programs and job requirements there. On a busy day at any dealership there will be several sales workers on the floor

Buyers

School Subjects	Business Mathematics
Personal Skills	Helping/teaching Leadership/management
Work Environment	Primarily indoors One location with some travel
Minimum Education Level	High school diploma
Salary Range	$18,000 to $28,500 to $63,000
Certification or Licensing	None available
Outlook	Little change or more slowly than the average

Overview

There are two main types of buyers: *Wholesale buyers* purchase merchandise directly from manufacturers and resell it to retail firms, commercial establishments, and other institutions; *retail buyers* purchase goods from wholesalers (and occasionally from manufacturers) for resale to the general public. In either case, buyers must understand their customers' needs and be able to purchase goods at an appropriate price and in sufficient quantity. Sometimes a buyer is referred to by the type of merchandise purchased—for example, jewelry buyer or toy buyer. *Government buyers* have similar responsibilities but need to be especially sensitive to concerns of fairness and ethics since they use public money to make their purchases.

History

The job of the buyer has been influenced by a variety of historical changes, including the growth of large retail stores in the 20th century. In the past, store owners typically performed almost all of the business activities, including the purchase of merchandise. Large stores, in contrast, had immensely more complicated operations, requiring large numbers of specialized workers, such as sales clerks, receiving and shipping clerks, advertising managers, personnel officers, and buyers. The introduction of mass production systems at factories required more complicated planning, ordering, and scheduling of purchases. A wider range of available merchandise also called for more astute selection and purchasing techniques.

The Job

Wholesale and retail buyers are part of a complex system of production, distribution, and merchandising. Both are concerned with recognizing and satisfying the huge variety of consumer needs and desires. Most specialize in acquiring one or two lines of merchandise.

Retail buyers work for retail stores. They generally can be divided into two types: The first, working directly under a merchandise manager, not only purchases goods but directly supervises salespeople. When a new product appears on the shelves, for example, buyers may work with salespeople to point out its distinctive features. This type of retail buyer thus takes responsibility for the products' marketing. The second type of retail buyer is concerned only with purchasing and has no supervisory responsibilities. These buyers cooperate with the sales staff to promote maximum sales.

All retail buyers must understand the basic merchandising policies of their stores. Purchases are affected by the size of the buyer's annual budget, the kind of merchandise needed in each buying season, and trends in the market. Success in buying is directly related to the profit or loss shown by particular departments. Buyers often work with *assistant buyers*, who spend much of their time maintaining sales and inventory records.

All buyers must be experts in the merchandise that they purchase. They order goods months ahead of their expected sale, and they must be able to predetermine salability based upon cost, style, and competitive items. Buyers must also be well acquainted with the best sources of supply for each product they purchase.

Depending upon the location, size, and type of store, a retail buyer may deal directly with traveling salespeople (ordering from samples or catalogs); order by mail or by telephone directly from the manufacturer or wholesaler; or travel to key cities to visit merchandise showrooms and manufacturing establishments. Most use a combination of these approaches.

Buying trips to such cities as New York, Chicago, and San Francisco are an important part of the work for buyers at a larger store. For specialized products, such as glassware, china, liquors, and gloves, some buyers make yearly trips to major European production centers. Sometimes manufacturers of similar items organize trade shows to attract a number of buyers. Buying trips are difficult; a buyer may visit six to eight suppliers in a single day. The buyer must make decisions on the spot about the opportunity for profitable sale of merchandise. The important element is not how much the buyer personally likes the merchandise but how much the customers will buy. Most buyers operate under an annual purchasing budget for the departments they represent.

Mergers between stores and expansion of individual department stores into chains of stores have created central buying positions. *Central buyers* order in unusually large quantities. As a result, they have the power to develop their own set of specifications for a particular item and ask manufacturers to bid on the right to provide it. Goods purchased by central buyers may be marketed under the manufacturer's label (as is normally done) or ordered with the store's label or a chain brand name.

To meet this competition, independent stores often work with *resident buyers*, who purchase merchandise for a large number of stores. By purchasing large quantities of the same product, resident buyers can obtain the same types of discounts enjoyed by large chain stores and then pass along the savings to their customers.

Because they work with public funds and must avoid any appearance of favoritism or corruption, government buyers sometimes purchase merchandise through open bids. The buyer may establish a specific set of specifications for a product and invite private firms to bid on the job. Some government buyers are required to accept the lowest bid. Each purchase must be well documented for public scrutiny. Like other types of buyers, government buyers must be well acquainted with the products they purchase, and they must try to find the best quality products for the lowest price.

Requirements

High School

A high school degree generally is required for entering the field of buying. Useful high school courses include mathematics, English, speech, and economics.

Postsecondary Training

A college degree is not usually a requirement for becoming a buyer, but it is becoming increasingly important, especially for advancement. A majority of buyers have attended college. Retailing experience also is helpful.

Training is available through trade associations, such as the National Association of Purchasing Management, which sponsors conferences, seminars, and workshops. Some colleges and universities also offer majors in purchasing or materials management. Useful college courses in preparation for a career in buying include accounting, economics, commercial law, finance, marketing, and various business classes, such as business communications, business organization and management, and computer applications in business.

Certification or Licensing

Certification, although not required, is becoming increasingly important. Various levels of certification are available through the American Purchasing Society and the National Association of Purchasing Management. To earn most certifications you must have work experience and fulfill education requirements, and pass written and oral exams.

Other Requirements

Important personal qualities are integrity, industriousness, and an ability to work well with people, to handle stress, and to make analytical judgments.

Exploring

One way to explore the retailing field is through part-time or summer employment in a store. A good time to look for such work is during the Christmas holiday season. Door-to-door selling is another way to gain retailing experience. Occasionally, experience in a retail store can be found through special high school programs.

Employers

Buyers work for a wide variety of businesses, both wholesale and retail, as well as for government agencies. Employers range from small stores, where buying may be only one function of a manager's job, to multinational corporations, where a buyer may specialize in one type of item and buy in enormous quantity.

Of the approximately 547,000 wholesale and retail buyers employed throughout the country in 1998, most worked for department stores, clothing stores, grocery stores, machinery wholesalers, electrical goods distributors, and grocery wholesalers. About half of buyers and purchasers worked in wholesale and retail trade businesses, while another one-fourth worked in manufacturing. Others worked in businesses that provide services and in government agencies.

Starting Out

Most buyers find their first job by applying to the personnel office of a retail establishment or wholesaler. Because knowledge of retailing is important, buyers may be required to have work experience in a store.

Most buyers begin their careers as retail sales workers. The next step may be *head of stock*. The head of stock maintains stock inventory records and keeps the merchandise in a neat and well-organized fashion both to protect its value and to permit easy access. He or she usually supervises the work of several employees. This person also works in an intermediate position between the salespeople on the floor and the buyer who provides the merchandise. The next step to becoming a buyer may be assistant buyer. For many department stores, promotion to full buyer requires this background.

Large department stores or chains operate executive training programs for college graduates who seek buying and other retail executive positions. A typical program consists of 16 successive weeks of work in a variety of departments. This on-the-job experience is supplemented by formal classroom work that most often is conducted by senior executives and training department personnel. Following this orientation, trainees are placed in junior management positions for an additional period of supervised experience and training.

Advancement

Buyers are key employees of the stores or companies that employ them. One way they advance is through increased responsibility, such as more authority to make commitments for merchandise and more complicated buying assignments.

Buyers are sometimes promoted to *merchandise manager*, which requires them to supervise other buyers, help develop the store's merchandising policies, and coordinate buying and selling activities with related departments. Other buyers may become vice presidents in charge of merchandising or even store presidents. Because buyers learn much about retailing in their job, they are in a position to advance to top executive positions. Some buyers use their knowledge of retailing and the contacts they have developed with suppliers to set up their own businesses.

Earnings

How much a buyer earns depends on various factors, including the employer's sales volume. Mass merchandisers, such as discount or chain department stores, pay among the highest salaries.

In 1998, earnings for buyers ranged from less than $17,730 for the lowest 10 percent to a high of $66,480 for the top 10 percent. Average salaries ranged from $23,490 to $42,920. In addition to their salaries, buyers often receive cash bonuses based on their performance and may be offered incentive plans, such as profit sharing and stock options. Most buyers receive the usual company benefits, such as vacation, sick leave, life and health insurance, and pension plans. They generally also receive an employee's discount of 10 to 20 percent on merchandise purchased for personal use.

Work Environment

Buyers work in a dynamic and sometimes stressful atmosphere. They must make important decisions on an hourly basis. The results of their work, both successes and failures, show up quickly on the profit and loss statement.

Buyers frequently work long or irregular hours. Evening and weekend hours are common, especially during the holiday season, when the retail field is at its busiest. Extra hours may be required to bring records up to date, for example, or to review stock and to become familiar with the store's over-all marketing design for the coming season. Travel may also be a regular part of a buyer's job, possibly requiring several days away from home each month.

Although buyers must sometimes work under pressure, they usually work in pleasant, well-lighted environments. They also benefit from having a diverse set of responsibilities.

Outlook

Prospects for buyers are expected to increase at a slower than average rate through 2008. The growth of branch stores is expected to create a demand for buyers, but this will be offset by other factors. Centralization of buying, as stores consolidate or participate in joint purchasing activities, may reduce the number of buyers needed, as will the increased use of computers, which allows buyers to do their jobs more efficiently. Competition will be keen because the field of merchandising is attractive to many college graduates, and job seekers can be expected to outnumber the opportunities available.

For More Information

For materials on educational programs in the retail industry, contact:

National Retail Federation
325 7th Street, NW, Suite 1100
Washington, DC 20004
Attn: Vice President of Research, Education and Community Affairs
Tel: 202-783-7971
Web: http://www.nrf.com/

For career information, send a request marked "Careers" to:

American Purchasing Society
30 West Downer Place
Aurora, IL 60506
Tel: 630-859-0250
Web: http://www.american-purchasing.com

For information on the magazine, Your Future Purchasing Career, *lists of colleges with purchasing programs, and bios of people in the field, contact:*

National Association of Purchasing Management
Customer Service
2055 East Centennial Circle
PO Box 22160
Tempe, AZ 85285
Tel: 800-888-6276, Ext. 401
Web: http://www.napm.org

For an information packet on purchasing careers in the government, contact:

National Institute of Government Purchasing, Inc.
151 Spring Street
Herndon, VA 20170-5223
Tel: 800-367-6447
Web: http://www.nigp.org

Cashiers

Business Mathematics	School Subjects
Following instructions Helping/teaching	Personal Skills
Primarily indoors Primarily one location	Work Environment
High school diploma	Minimum Education Level
$8,500 to $12,000 to $27,900	Salary Range
None available	Certification or Licensing
About as fast as the average	Outlook

Overview

Cashiers are employed in many different businesses, including supermarkets, department stores, restaurants, and movie theaters. In general, they are responsible for handling money received from customers.

One of the principal tasks of a cashier is operating a cash register. The cash register records all the monetary transactions going into or out of the cashier's workstation. These transactions might involve cash, credit card charges, personal checks, refunds, and exchanges. To assist in inventory control, the cash register often tallies the specific products that are sold.

History

In earlier times, when most stores were small and independently owned, merchants were usually able to take care of most aspects of their businesses, including receiving money from customers. The demand for cashiers increased as large department stores, supermarkets, and self-service stores became more common. Cashiers were hired to receive customers' money, make change, provide customer receipts, and wrap merchandise. Cashiers, who dealt with customers one-on-one, also became the primary representatives of these businesses.

The Job

Although cashiers are employed in many different types of businesses and establishments, most handle the following tasks: receiving money from customers, making change, and providing customers with a payment receipt. The type of business dictates other duties. In supermarkets, for example, they might be required to bag groceries. Typically, cashiers in drug or department stores also package or bag merchandise for customers. In currency exchanges, they cash checks, receive utility bill payments, and sell various licenses and permits.

At some businesses, cashiers handle tasks not directly related to customers. Some cashiers, for example, prepare bank deposits for the management. In large businesses, where cashiers are often given a lot of responsibility, they may receive and record cash payments made to the firm and handle payment of the firm's bills. Cashiers might even prepare sales tax reports, compute income tax deductions for employees' pay rates, and prepare paychecks and payroll envelopes.

Cashiers usually operate some type of cash register or other business machine. These machines might print out the amount of each purchase, automatically add the total amount, provide a paper receipt for the customer, and open the cash drawer for the cashier. Other, more complex machines, such as those used in hotels, large department stores, and supermarkets, might print out an itemized bill of the customer's purchases. In some cases, cashiers use electronic devices called optical scanners, which read the prices of goods from bar codes printed on the merchandise. As the cashier passes the product over the scanner, the scanner reads the code on the product and transmits the code to the cashier's terminal. The price of the item is then automatically displayed at the terminal and added to the customer's bill. Cashiers generally have their own drawer of money, known as a *bank*, which fits into the cash register or terminal. They must keep an accurate record of the amount of money in the drawer. Other machines that are used by cashiers include adding machines and change-dispensing machines.

Job titles vary depending on where the cashier is employed. In supermarkets, cashiers might be known as *check-out clerks* or *grocery checkers*; in utility companies they are typically called *bill clerks* or *tellers*; in theaters they are often referred to as *ticket sellers* or *box office cashiers*; and in cafeterias they are frequently called *cashier-checkers, food checkers,* or *food tabulators.* In large businesses, cashiers might be given special job titles such as *disbursement clerk, credit cashier,* or *cash accounting clerk.*

In addition to handling money, theater box office cashiers might answer telephone inquiries and operate machines that dispense tickets and change. Restaurant cashiers might receive telephone calls for meal reservations and for special parties, keep the reservation book current, type the menu, stock the sales counter with candies and smoking supplies, and seat customers.

Department store or supermarket cashiers typically bag or wrap purchases. During slack periods they might price the merchandise, restock shelves, make out order forms, and perform other duties similar to those of *food and beverage order clerks.* Those employed as hotel cashiers usually keep accurate records of telephone charges and room-service bills to go on the customer's account. They might also be in charge of overseeing customers' safe-deposit boxes, handling credit card billing, and notifying *room clerks* of customer checkouts.

Cashier supervisors, money-room supervisors, and *money counters* might act as cashiers for other cashiers—receiving and recording cash and sales slips from them and making sure their cash registers contain enough money to make change for customers. Other cashier positions include *gambling cashiers,* who buy and sell chips for cash; *pari-mutuel ticket cashiers and sellers,* who buy and sell betting tickets at racetracks; *paymasters of purses,* who are responsible for collecting money for and paying money to racehorse owners; and *auction clerks,* who are responsible for collecting money from winning bidders at auctions.

Requirements

Some employers require that cashiers be at least 18 years old and have graduated from high school. Employers might also prefer applicants with previous job experience, the ability to type, or knowledge of elementary accounting. Cashiers typically receive on-the-job training from experienced employees. In addition, some businesses have special training programs, providing information on the store's history, for example, as well as instruction on store procedures, security measures, and the use of equipment.

High School

High school courses useful to cashiers include bookkeeping, typing, business machine operation, and business arithmetic.

Postsecondary Training

For some kinds of more complicated cashier jobs, employers might prefer applicants who are graduates of a two-year community college or business school. Businesses often fill cashier positions by promoting existing employees, such as clerk-typists, baggers, and ushers.

Other Requirements

Most cashiers have constant personal contact with the public. A pleasant disposition and a desire to serve the public are thus important qualities. Cashiers must also be proficient with numbers and have good hand-eye coordination and finger dexterity. Accuracy is especially important.

Because they handle large sums of money, some cashiers must be able to meet the standards of bonding companies. Bonding companies evaluate applicants for risks and frequently fingerprint applicants for registration and background checks. Not all cashiers are required to be bonded, however.

In some areas, cashiers are required to join a union, but fewer than 20 percent of cashiers are union members. Most union cashiers work in grocery stores and supermarkets and belong to the United Food and Commercial Workers International Union.

Exploring

You can try to find part-time employment as a cashier. This will enable you to explore your interest and aptitude for this type of work. You can sometimes obtain related job experience by working in the school bookstore or cafeteria or by participating in community activities, such as raffles and sales drives that require the handling of money. It can also be useful to talk with persons already employed as cashiers.

Employers

Most cashiers work in supermarkets and grocery stores. Large numbers are also employed in department, drug, shoe, and other retail stores, and many work in restaurants, hotels, theaters, and hospitals.

Starting Out

People generally enter this field by applying directly to the personnel directors of large businesses or to the managers or owners of small businesses. Applicants may learn of job openings through newspaper help wanted ads, through friends and business associates, or through school placement agencies. Private or state employment agencies can also help. Employers sometimes require that applicants provide personal references from schools or former employers attesting to their character and personal qualifications.

Advancement

Opportunities for advancement vary depending on the size and type of business, personal initiative, experience, and special training and skills. Cashier positions, for example, can provide people with the business skills to move into other types of clerical jobs or managerial positions. Opportunities for promotion are greater within larger firms than in small businesses or stores. Cashiers sometimes advance to cashier supervisors, shift leaders, division managers, or store managers. In hotels, they might be able to advance to room clerks or related positions.

Earnings

New cashiers with no experience are generally paid the minimum wage. Employers can pay workers younger than 20 a lower training wage for up to six months.

The median annual salary for cashiers, according to the *Occupational Outlook Handbook*, is about $12,844. Most cashiers earn between $10,296 and $17,056 a year. Wages are generally higher for union workers, however. Experienced, full-time cashiers belonging to the United Food and Commercial Workers International Union average about $27,900 a year; beginners make much less, averaging about $5.90 per hour. Cashiers employed in restaurants generally earn less than those in other businesses do.

Some cashiers, especially those working for large companies, receive health and life insurance as well as paid vacations and sick days. Some are also offered employee retirement plans or stock option plans. Cashiers are sometimes given merchandise discounts. Benefits are usually available only to full-time employees. Some employers try to save money by hiring part-time cashiers and not paying them benefits.

Work Environment

Cashiers sometimes work evenings, weekends, and holidays, when many people shop and go out for entertainment. The work of the cashier is usually not too strenuous, but employees often need to stand during most of their working hours. Cashiers must be able to work rapidly and under pressure during rush hours.

Most cashiers work indoors and in rooms that are well ventilated and well lighted. The work area itself, however, can be rather small and confining; cashiers typically work behind counters, in cages or booths, or in other small spaces. Work spaces for cashiers are frequently located near entrances and exits, so cashiers may be exposed to drafts.

Outlook

There are more than 3.2 million cashiers in the United States, although more than half of them work part time. This occupation is expected to grow as fast as the average through 2008. Due to a high turnover rate among cashiers, many jobs will become available as workers leaving the field are replaced. Each year almost one-third of all cashiers leave their jobs for various reasons.

Cashier positions increased greatly during the 1970s and 1980s as businesses turned to modern merchandising methods, such as an emphasis on self-service. Most businesses likely to turn to self-service have already done so, however, and the growth in opportunities resulting from this change is expected to be minor.

Factors that could limit job growth include the increased installation of automatic change-making machines, vending machines, and other types of automatic and electronic equipment, which could decrease the number of cashiers needed in some business operations. Future job opportunities will be available to those experienced in bookkeeping, typing, business machine operation, and general office skills. Many part-time jobs should also be available. Although the majority of cashiers employed are 24 years of age or younger, many businesses have started hiring the elderly to fill some job openings.

For More Information

For information about educational programs in the retail industry, contact:

National Retail Federation
325 7th Street, NW, Suite 1100
Washington, DC 20004
Tel: 202-783-7971
Web: http://www.nrf.com

Computer and Electronics Sales Representatives

School Subjects	Business Computer science Speech
Personal Skills	Communication/ideas Technical/scientific
Work Environment	Primarily indoors Primarily multiple locations
Minimum Education Level	Bachelor's degree
Salary Range	$11,000 to $52,000 to $100,000+
Certification or Licensing	None available
Outlook	Little change or more slowly than the average

Overview

Computer and electronics sales representatives sell hardware, software, peripheral computer equipment, and electronics equipment to customers and businesses of all sizes. Sometimes they follow up sales with installation of systems, maintenance, or training of the client's staff. They are employed in all aspects of businesses. Sales representatives that work for retail stores deal with consumers. Representatives that specialize in a particular piece of hardware, certain software program, or electronic component may do business with banks, insurance companies, or accounting firms, among others.

History

The first major advances in modern computer technology were made during World War II. After the war, people thought that computers were too big (they easily filled entire warehouses) to ever be used for anything other than government projects, such as their use in compiling the 1950 census.

The introduction of semiconductors to computer technology made smaller and less expensive computers possible. The semiconductors replaced the bigger, slower vacuum tubes of the first computers. These changes made it easier for businesses to adapt computers to their needs, which they began doing as early as 1954. Within 30 years, computers had revolutionized the way people work, play, and even shop. Few occupations have remained untouched by this technological revolution. Consequently, computers are found in businesses, government offices, hospitals, schools, science labs, and homes. Clearly, there is a huge market for the sale of computers and peripheral equipment. There is an important need today for knowledgeable sales representatives to serve both the retail public and to advise corporations and large organizations on their computer and electronics purchases.

The Job

The first step in the selling process, no matter the sale environment—retail or corporate—is client consultation. Sales representatives determine the client's current technological needs, as well as those of the future. During consultation, reps explain the technology's value and how well it will perform. Often, customers do not have expertise in computer or electronics technology, so the rep must explain and translate complicated computer tech-talk, as well as answer numerous questions. In retail computer sales, the customer decides what system, peripheral, or software to purchase and then brings it home or arranges for its delivery.

In the corporate sales environment, client consultations usually take longer, often entailing numerous trips to the client's office or place of business. Ron Corrales, an Account Support Manager for Andersen Consulting, acknowledges client consultation is the crucial first step in the sales process. After the client's business is researched and their needs assessed, possible solutions are outlined in the form of a written or oral presentation. "I was really nervous the first few times I gave a presentation," recalls Corrales. "After all, these were CEOs and CFOs of Fortune 500 companies!" The talent for public speaking and technical writing frequently comes into play.

Sales representatives must be able to effectively and clearly present the product and its capabilities, often in layperson's terms. After perfecting his communications skills, Corrales now thinks of client presentations as "just part of the job."

Andersen Consulting (AC) is the largest information technology (IT) consulting firm in the world. They provide proprietary software used by businesses worldwide. Their programs are tailored to fit the needs of each company and their specific routines, such as accounting, customer billing, inventory control, and marketing, among others. Their client list includes the grocery store chain, Kroger's, Harley Davidson, and the U.S. government.

After the presentation, if all goes well, Corrales helps draft the contract. Every aspect of the agreement is outlined and specified—the type of software, length of contract, including services, training, or maintenance. The deal is considered "done" once the AC partners and company CEOs sign, and of course, the fees are paid. Once the companies receive their software, it is installed and glitches, if any, are resolved. Many times company employees are trained by AC consultants on how to use the software to its fullest capability. Usually, a one-year maintenance contract is provided to the client.

To stay abreast of technological advances, sales representatives must attend training sessions or continuing education classes. It also helps to know the essence of each client's field and the nature of their work. Weekly departmental meetings are necessary to know of any developments or projects within the department, or AC as a whole. A big part of Corrales's job is managing his territory, making client calls, or visits when necessary. A chunk of his work day is devoted to "putting out potential client 'fires'."

Requirements

High School

Classes in speech and writing will help you learn how to communicate your product to large groups of people. Computer science and electronics classes will give you a basic overview of the field. General business and math classes will also be helpful.

Postsecondary Training

Though a small number of computer sales positions may be filled by high school graduates, those jobs are scarce. Most large companies prefer a bachelor's or advanced degree in computer science or related background, marketing, or business.

Prepare yourself for a career in this field by developing your computer knowledge—take computer and math classes, as well as business classes to help develop a sound business sense. Since sales representatives are often required to meet with clients and make sales presentations, excellent communications skills are a must. Hone yours by taking English and speech classes.

In this particular field of sales, extensive computer knowledge is just as important as business savvy. Most computer sales representatives pursue computer science courses concurrently with their business classes. For computer sales representatives specializing in a specific industry, say health care or banking, training in the basics and current issues of that field is needed. Such training can be obtained through special work training seminars, adult education classes, or courses at a technical school. Many companies require their sales staff to complete a training program where they'll learn the technologies and work tools needed for the job. (This is where you'll pick up the techno-speak for your specific field.)

Corrales holds a Master of Information Science degree. One of the college classes that has helped him the most in his career is "technical writing and communication—it helps to be able to explain complicated and technical material in layperson terms."

Other Requirements

Equally important as formal education and computer and electronics knowledge is having a "sales" personality. Sales representatives must be confident and knowledgeable about themselves as well as the product they are selling. They should have strong interpersonal skills and enjoy dealing with all types of people—from families buying their first PC, to CEOs of a Fortune 500 company. "People in this business are well rounded and enjoy technology," Corrales adds, "but, to do well, they need to be competitively hungry, and like to talk—a lot!"

Employers

Employment opportunities for this field exist nationwide. What are your priorities? Do you want to work for an industry giant? IBM? Microsoft? Motorola? You may be enticed with attractive perks—stock options, big travel expense account, graduate school tuition, among other benefits. Note, however, that these are huge corporations; you'll really have to be something special if you want to stand apart from the other applicants. Getting hired is tough, too. Microsoft, for example, receives thousands of resumes weekly.

Middle-size and small companies usually require their employees to don several hats. Sales representatives may be responsible for entire presentations, including product and client research, as well as maintenance and service. It may sound like much work, and maybe for some tasks you may feel over-qualified. The rewards include being part of the ground team when your company takes off. If it doesn't, you can always chalk it up to good experience.

Starting Out

That Corrales had two job offers by graduation is not uncommon, especially for students with computer related majors. Many top companies aggressively recruit on campus, often enticing soon-to-be grads with signing bonuses or other incentives at school sponsored job fairs.

Other avenues to try when conducting your job search include the newspaper job ads and trade papers. Try the Internet, too. Many companies maintain Web sites where they post employment opportunities as well as receive online resumes and applications. Your school's job placement center is a great place to start your job search. Not only will the counselors have information on jobs not advertised in the paper, but they can provide tips on resume writing and interviewing techniques.

Advancement

With a good work record, a computer or electronics sales representative may be offered a position in management. A manager is responsible for supervising the sales for a given retail store, sales territory, or corporate branch. A management position not only comes with a higher salary, but a higher level of responsibility as well. An effective manager should be well versed in the company's product, sales techniques, and be able to keep a sales group working at top capacity. Those already at the management level may decide to transfer to the marketing side of the business. Positions in marketing may involve planning the marketing strategy for a new computer or electronics product or line, and coordinatiing sales campaigns and product distribution.

Earnings

There is great variance regarding annual salaries for this field. Electronics and computer sales representatives working in retail are paid an hourly wage—usually minimum wage, $5.15 an hour—supplemented with commissions based on a percentage of sales made that day or week. Median annual earnings of sales representatives, except retail, were $36,540, including comission, in 1998, according to the *Occupational Outlook Handbook*. Top salaries were more than $83,000.

Computer sales representatives specializing in corporate sales of hardware or software tend to earn quite a bit more. First, corporate sales people usually hold a college degree. They also deal with larger sales packages that mean larger commissions. According to a recent WetFeet.com industry study, sales associates specializing in hardware components averaged between $30,000 to $40,000 base salary; commissions raised the final averages to between $45,000 to $60,000 a year. Salaries are dependent on the product sold—PCs, mainframes, peripherals—and the market served.

A 1998 international sales and marketing salary survey conducted by Sales & Marketing Executives International pegged annual salaries a bit higher. Experienced account representatives in the computer/information field earned an annual salary of about $52,000; sales managers earned about $75,000; and marketing managers earned $104,125. (Year-end bonuses are often given to employees, greatly enhancing their final yearly salary.)

Most computer sales representatives are offered a benefit package including health and life insurance, paid holidays and vacations, continuing education and training, as well as volume bonuses or stock options.

Work Environment

Retail sales representatives work in a retail environment. A 40-hour work-week is typical, though longer hours may be necessary during busy shopping seasons. Whether or not the sales representative is compensated during these extended hours varies from store to store. However, increased work times usually means increased sales volume, which in the end, translates to more commissions. Retail representatives must be prepared to deal with a large volume of customers with varying levels of technical knowledge, all with many questions. It is necessary to treat customers with respect and patience, regardless of the size of the sale—or if a sale is made at all.

Corporate sales representatives, like Corrales, work in a professional office environment. Work is conducted at the home office, as well as in the field when making sales calls. Work schedules vary depending on the size of territory and number of clients. A 40-hour workweek is the exception, rather than the rule. "I average about 60+ hours a week," says Corrales. "My hours are flexible, but with a lot of weekend work and travel."

Also, corporate sales representatives should have excellent communications skills—both in person and on the telephone—as they spend a lot of time consulting with clients. Also, good writing skills are needed when producing proposals and sales reports, often under the pressure of a tight deadline.

Outlook

Employment opportunities for all sales representatives are expected to grow more slowly than the average through 2008. Retail sales representatives should see employment opportunities grow about as fast as the average. As computer companies continue to price their products competitively, more and more people will be able to afford a new home computer system, or upgrade existing ones with the latest hardware, software, and peripherals. Increased retail sales will warrant competent and knowledgeable sales representatives. Many jobs exist at retail giants (Best Buy and Office Depot, known for office related supplies and equipment, are two examples) that provide consumers with good price packages as well as optional services such as installation and maintenance.

Employment opportunities can also be found with computer specialty stores or consulting companies that deal directly with businesses and their corporate computer and application needs. Computers have become an almost indispensable tool for running a successful business be it an accounting firm, public relations company, or a multi-physician medical practice. As long as this trend continues, knowledgeable sales representatives will be needed to bring the latest technological advances in hardware and software to the consumer and corporate level.

For More Information

For industry or membership information, contact:

National Association of Retail Dealers of America
10 East 22nd Street
Lombard, IL 60148-4915
Tel: 630-953-8950
Email: nardahdq@aol.com
Web: http://www.narda.com

Contact ACM for information on internships, student membership, and the ACM student magazine, **Crossroads.** *ACM also offers a student Web site at http://www.acm.org/membership/student/.*

Association for Computing Machinery (ACM)
1515 Broadway
New York, NY 10036-5701
Tel: 212-869-7440
Email: SIGS@acm.org
Web: http://www.acm.org

The Electronics Representatives Association is the trade organization of professional sales and marketing companies that specialize in multiple-line selling of computers, software, and other electronic products. For industry and membership information, or for a copy of **The Representor,** *a quarterly trade magazine, contact:*

The Electronics Representatives Association
444 North Michigan Avenue, Suite 1960
Chicago, IL 60611
Tel: 312-527-3050
Email: info@era.org
Web: http://www.era.org

Counter and Retail Clerks

————School Subjects

English
Mathematics
Speech

————Personal Skills

Following instructions
Helping/teaching

————Work Environment

Primarily indoors
Primarily one location

————Minimum Education Level

High school diploma

————Salary Range

$8,840 to $13,100 to $26,700

————Certification or Licensing

None available

————Outlook

Faster than the average

Overview

Counter and retail clerks work as intermediaries between the general public and businesses that provide goods and services. They take orders and receive payments for such services as videotape rentals, automobile rentals, and laundry and dry cleaning. They often assist customers with their purchasing or rental decisions, especially when sales personnel are not available. They might also prepare billing statements, keep records of receipts and sales, and balance money in their cash registers.

History

The first retail outlets in the United States sold food staples, farm necessities, and clothing, and many also served as the post office and became the social and economic centers of their communities. Owners of these general stores often performed all the jobs in the business.

Over the years retailing has undergone numerous changes. Large retail stores, requiring many workers, including counter and retail clerks, became more common. Also emerging were specialized retail or chain outlets—clothing stores, bicycle shops, computer shops, video stores, and athletic footwear boutiques—which also needed counter and retail clerks to assist customers and to receive payment for services or products.

The Job

Job duties vary depending on the type of business. In a shoe repair shop, for example, the clerk receives the shoes to be repaired or cleaned from the customer, examines the shoes, gives a price quote and a receipt to the customer, and then sends the shoes to the work department for the necessary repairs or cleaning. The shoes are marked with a tag specifying what work needs to be done and to whom the shoes belong. After the work is completed, the clerk returns the shoes to the customer and collects payment.

In stores where customers rent equipment or merchandise, clerks prepare rental forms and quote rates to customers. The clerks answer customer questions about the operation of the equipment. They often take a deposit to cover any accidents or possible damage. Clerks also check the equipment to be certain it is in good working order and make minor adjustments, if necessary. With long-term rentals, such as storage-facility rentals, clerks notify the customers when the rental period is about to expire and when the rent is overdue. *Video-rental clerks* greet customers, check out tapes, and accept payment. Upon return of the tapes, the clerks check the condition of the tapes and then put them back on the shelves.

In smaller shops with no sales personnel or in situations when the sales personnel are unavailable, counter and retail clerks assist customers with purchases or rentals by demonstrating the merchandise, answering customers' questions, accepting payment, recording sales, and wrapping the purchases or arranging for their delivery.

In addition to these duties, clerks sometimes prepare billing statements to be sent to customers. They might keep records of receipts and sales throughout the day and balance the money in their registers when their work shift ends. They sometimes are responsible for the display and presentation of products in their store. In supermarkets and grocery stores, clerks stock shelves and bag food purchases for the customers.

Service-establishment attendants work in various types of businesses, such as a laundry, where attendants take clothes to be cleaned or repaired and write down the customer's name and address. *Watch-and-clock-repair clerks* receive clocks and watches for repair and examine the timepieces to estimate repair costs. They might make minor repairs, such as replacing a watchband; otherwise, the timepiece is forwarded to the repair shop with a description of needed repairs.

Many clerks have job titles that describe what they do and where they work. These include laundry-pricing clerks, telegraph-counter clerks, photo-finishing-counter clerks, tool-and-equipment-rental clerks, airplane-charter clerks, baby-stroller and wheelchair-rental clerks, storage-facility-rental clerks, boat-rental clerks, hospital-television-rental clerks, trailer-rental clerks, automobile-rental clerks, fur-storage clerks, and self-service-laundry and dry-cleaning attendants.

Requirements

Although there are no specific educational requirements for clerk positions, most employers prefer to hire high school graduates. Legible handwriting and the ability to add and subtract numbers quickly are also necessary.

High School

High school courses useful for the job include English, speech, and mathematics, as well as any business-related classes, such as typing and those covering principles in retailing.

Other Requirements

Counter and retail clerks should have a pleasant personality and an ability to interact with a variety of people. They should also be neat and well groomed and have a high degree of personal responsibility. Counter and retail clerks must be able to adjust to alternating periods of heavy and light activity. No two days—or even customers—are alike. Because some customers can be rude or even hostile, clerks must exercise tact and patience at all times.

Exploring

There are numerous opportunities for part-time or temporary work as a clerk, especially during the holiday season. Many high schools have developed work-study programs that combine courses in retailing with part-time work in the field. Store owners cooperating in these programs often hire these students as full-time workers after they complete the course.

Employers

Counter and retail clerks are employed in countless types of establishments: laundries and dry cleaners, hardware stores, automobile rental firms, supermarkets and grocery stores, video rental stores, and other rental services—in fact, nearly anywhere that goods are sold or services provided to the general public.

Starting Out

Those interested in securing an entry-level position as a clerk should contact stores directly. Workers with some experience, such as those who have completed a work-study program in high school, should have the greatest success, but most entry-level positions do not require any previous experience. Jobs are often listed in help-wanted advertisements.

Most stores provide new workers with on-the-job training in which experienced clerks explain company policies and procedures and teach new employees how to operate the cash register and other necessary equipment. This training usually continues for several weeks until the new employee feels comfortable on the job.

Advancement

Counter and retail clerks usually begin their employment doing routine tasks, such as checking stock and operating the cash register. With experience they might advance to more complicated assignments and assume some sales responsibilities. Those with the skill and aptitude might become *salespeople* or *store managers*, although further education is normally required for management positions.

The high turnover rate in the clerk position increases the opportunities for being promoted. The number and kind of opportunities, however, depend on the place of employment and the ability, training, and experience of the employee.

Earnings

Beginning counter and retail clerks in 1999 generally earned about the minimum wage. Experienced clerks average between $6 an hour and $8.79 an hour, with some making as much as $11.12 an hour. The highest wages are paid to those with the greatest number of job responsibilities.

According to the *Occupational Outlook Handbook,* full-time clerks averaged about $278 a week, or $14,497 annually. Clerks with considerable work experience earned about $631 weekly, or $32,812 a year. Those workers who have union affiliation (usually those who work for supermarkets) may earn considerably more than their nonunion counterparts. Full-time workers, especially those who are union members, might also receive benefits such as paid vacation time and health insurance, but this is not the industry norm. Some businesses offer merchandise discounts for their employees. Part-time workers usually receive fewer benefits than those working full-time.

Work Environment

Although a 40-hour workweek is common, many stores operate on a 44- to 48-hour workweek. Most stores are open on Saturday and many on Sunday. Most stores are also open one or more weekday evenings, so a clerk's working hours might vary from week to week and include evening and weekend shifts. Many counter and retail clerks work overtime during Christmas and other rush seasons. Part-time clerks generally work during peak business periods.

Most clerks work indoors in well-ventilated and well-lighted environments. The job can be routine and repetitive, and clerks often spend much of their time on their feet.

Outlook

Approximately 469,000 people were employed as retail and counter clerks in the United States in 1998. About half worked part-time. Because of the proliferation of retail outlets, job opportunities for counter and retail clerks are expected to grow faster than average through 2008.

As is currently the case, major employers will be laundry or dry-cleaning establishments, automobile rental firms, and supermarkets and grocery stores. The continued growth in video rental stores and other rental services will also increase the need for skilled clerks. There should also be an increase in the number of opportunities for temporary or part-time work, especially during busy business periods. However, due to the high turnover rate of this field, most job openings will result from the need to replace workers. Employment opportunities for clerks are plentiful in large metropolitan areas, where their services are in great demand.

For More Information

For information about educational programs in the retail industry, contact:

National Retail Federation
325 7th Street, NW, Suite 1000
Washington, DC 20004
Tel: 202-783-7971
Web: http://www.nrf.com

Customer Service Representatives

	School Subjects
Business	
English	
Speech	

	Personal Skills
Communication/ideas	
Helping/teaching	

	Work Environment
Primarily indoors	
Primarily one location	

	Minimum Education Level
High school diploma	

	Salary Range
$18,000 to $26,075 to $32,000	

	Certification or Licensing
None available	

	Outlook
About as fast as the average	

Overview

Customer service representatives, sometimes called *customer care representatives*, work with customers of one or many companies, assist with customer problems, or answer questions. Customer service representatives work in many different industries to provide "front-line" customer service in a variety of businesses. Most customer service representatives work in an office setting though some may work in the "field" to better meet customer needs.

History

Customer service has been a part of business for many years; however, the formal title of customer service representative is relatively new. It was a little over 10 years ago that the International Customer Service Association established Customer Service Week to recognize and promote customer service.

In 1992, President George Bush (born 1924) made the week a national event. "If the United States is to remain a leader in the changing global economy, highest quality customer service must be a personal goal of every employee in business and industry," said the president in his proclamation.

As the world moves to a more global and competitive economic market, customer service, along with quality, has taken a front seat in the business world. Serving the customer and serving them well is more important now than ever before.

Customer service is about communication, so the progress in customer service can be tied closely to the progress in the communication industry. When Alexander Graham Bell (1847-1922) invented the telephone in 1876, he probably did not envision the customer service lines, automated response messages, and toll-free phone numbers that now help customer service representatives do their jobs.

The increased use of the Internet has helped companies serve and communicate with their customers in another way. From the simple email complaint form to online help files, companies are using the Internet to provide better customer service. Some companies even have online chat capabilities to communicate with their customers instantaneously on the Web.

The Job

Julie Cox is a customer service representative for Affina. Affina is a call center that handles customer service for a variety of companies. Cox works with each of Affina's clients and the call center operators to ensure that each call-in receives top customer service.

Customer service representatives often handle complaints and problems, and Cox finds that to be the case at the call center as well. While the operators who report to her are working on providing customer service to those on the phone, Cox must oversee that customer service while also keeping in mind the customer service for her client, whatever business they may be in.

"I make sure that the clients get regular reports of the customer service calls and check to see if there are any recurring problems," she says.

One of the ways Cox observes if customer service is not being handled effectively is by monitoring the actual time spent on each phone call. If an operator spends a lot of time on a call, there is most likely a problem.

"Our customers are billed per minute," says Cox. "So we want to make sure their customer service is being handled well and efficiently."

Affina's call center in Columbus, Indiana, handles dozens of toll-free lines. While some calls are likely to be focused on complaints or questions, some are easier to handle. Cox and her staff handle calls from people simply wanting to order literature, brochures, or to find their nearest dealer location.

Customer service representatives work in a variety of fields and business, but one thing is common—the customer. All businesses depend on their customers to keep them in business, so customer service, whether handled internally or outsourced to a call center like Affina, is extremely important.

Some customer service representatives, like Cox, do most of their work on the telephone. Others may represent companies in the field, where the customer is actually using the product or service. Still other customer service representatives may specialize in Internet service, assisting customers over the World Wide Web via email or online chats.

Affina's call center is available to their clients 24 hours a day, seven days a week, so Cox and her staff must keep around-the-clock shifts. Not all customer service representatives work a varied schedule; many work a traditional daytime shift. However, customers have problems, complaints, and questions 24 hours a day, so many companies do staff their customer service positions for a longer number of hours, especially to accommodate customers during evenings and weekends.

Requirements

High School

A high school diploma is required for most customer service representatives. High school courses that emphasize communication, such as English and speech, will help you learn to communicate clearly. Any courses that require collaboration with others will also help to teach diplomacy and tact—two important aspects of customer service. Business courses will help you get a good overview of the business world, one that is dependent on customers and customer service.

Postsecondary Training

While a college degree is not necessary to become a customer service representative, certain areas of postsecondary training are helpful. Courses in business and organizational leadership will help to give you a better feel for the business world. Just as in high school, communications classes are helpful in learning to effectively talk with and meet the needs of other people.

These courses can be taken during a college curriculum or may be offered at a variety of customer service workshops or classes. Cox is working as a customer service representative while she earns her business degree from a local college. Along with her college work, she has taken advantage of seminars and workshops to improve her customer service skills.

Other Requirements

"The best and the worst part of being a customer service representative are the people," Cox says. Customer service representatives should have the ability to maintain a pleasant attitude at all times, even while serving angry or demanding customers.

A successful customer service representative will most likely have an outgoing personality and enjoy working with people and assisting them with their questions and problems.

Because many customer service representatives work in offices and on the telephone, people with physical disabilities may find this career to be both accessible and enjoyable.

Exploring

Cox first discovered her love for customer service while working in retail at a local department store. Explore your ability for customer service by getting a job that deals with the public on a day-to-day basis. Talk with someone who works with customers and customer service every day; find out what they like and dislike about their jobs.

Evaluate the customer service at the businesses you visit. What makes that salesperson at The Gap better than the operator you talked with last week? Volunteer to answer phones at an agency in your town or city. Most receptionists in small companies and agencies are called on to provide customer service to callers. Try a nonprofit organization. They will welcome the help, and you will get a firsthand look at customer service.

Employers

Customer service representatives are hired at all types of companies in a variety of areas. Because all businesses rely on customers, customer service is generally a high priority for those businesses. Some companies, like call centers, may employ a large number of customer service representatives to serve a multitude of clients, while small businesses may simply have one or two people who are responsible for customer service.

Geography makes little difference when it comes to customer service. Smaller businesses may not be able to hire a person to handle customer service exclusively, but most businesses will have people designated to meet customer's needs.

Starting Out

You can become a customer service representative as an entry-level applicant, although some customer service representatives have first served in other areas of a company. This company experience may provide them with more knowledge and experience to answer customer questions. A college degree is not required, but any postsecondary training will increase your ability to find a job in customer service.

Customer service job openings are readily available in newspaper ads and on Internet job search sites. With some experience and a positive attitude, it is possible to move into the position of customer service representative from another job within the company. Cox started out at Affina as an operator and quickly moved into a customer service capacity.

Advancement

Customer service experience is valuable in any business career path. Cox hopes to combine her customer service experience with a business degree and move to the human resources area of her company.

It is also possible to advance to management or marketing jobs after working as a customer service representative. Businesses and their customers are inseparable, so most business professionals are experts at customer relations.

Earnings

In the Customer Care Institute's 1997 salary survey, customer service representatives reported average earnings of $26,075 per year. Entry-level representatives started as low as $18,000 per year, with experienced customer service representatives earning up to $32,000 per year.

Other benefits vary widely according to the size and type of company in which representatives are employed. Benefits may include medical, dental, vision, and life insurance, 401K plans, or bonus incentives. Full-time customer service representatives can expect to receive vacation and sick pay, while part-time workers may not be offered these benefits.

Work Environment

Customer service representatives work primarily indoors, although some may work in the field where the customers are using the product or service. They usually work in a supervised setting and report to a manager. They may spend many hours on the telephone, answering mail, or handling Internet communication. Many of the work hours involve little physical activity.

While most customer service representatives generally work a 40-hour workweek, others work a variety of shifts. Many businesses want customer service hours to coincide with the times that their customers are available to call or contact the business. For many companies, these times are in the evenings and on the weekends, so some customer service representatives work a varied shift and odd hours.

Outlook

The U.S. Department of Labor predicts that employment for customer service representatives will grow about as fast as the average for all other occupations. While businesses are growing and customers continue to need contact with those businesses, some growth in this field will be offset by growing technological trends. Customer relations handled via the Internet or automated answering machines will eliminate the need for growth in some areas.

For customer service representatives with specific knowledge of a product or business, the outlook is very good, as quick, efficient customer service is valuable in any business. Additional training and education will also make finding a job as a customer service representative an easier task.

For More Information

For information on customer service and other support positions, contact:

The Association of Support Professionals
66 Mt. Auburn Street
Watertown, MA 02472
Tel: 617-924-3944
Email: asp@softletter.com
Web: http://www.asponline.com

For information on jobs, training, workshops, and salaries, contact:

Customer Care Institute
17 Dean Overlook, NW
Atlanta, GA 30318
Tel: 404-352-9291
Email: info@customercare.com
Web: http://www.customercare.com

For information about the customer service industry, contact:

Help Desk Institute
5475 Tech Center Drive, Suite 210
Colorado Springs, CO 80919
Tel: 800-248-5667
Email: CSSC@zd.com
Web: http://www.helpdeskinst.com

For more information on international customer service careers, contact:

International Customer Service Association
401 North Michigan Avenue, Suite 2200
Chicago, IL 60611-4267
Tel: 800-360-4272
Email: icsa@sba.com
Web: http://www.icsa.com

Florists

Overview

Floral designers, or *florists,* arrange live or cut flowers, potted plants, foliage, or other decorative items, according to basic design principles to make eye pleasing creations. Designers make such arrangements for birthdays, weddings, funerals, or other occasions. They are employed by small local flower shops or larger national chains, grocery stores, or established at-home businesses. There are over 200,000 floral design workers employed in the United States.

History

Flowers have been used for centuries as decoration, personal adornment, or for religious significance. Ancient Egyptians used flowers to honor their many gods and goddesses. Flowers were arranged in low bowls in an orderly, repetitive pattern—flower, bud, foliage, and so on. Special spouted vases were also used to hold flowers. Lotus flowers, also called water lilies, were Egyptian favorites. They came to symbolize sacredness, and were associated with Isis, the Egyptian nature goddess. Flowers were sometimes used as decorations for the body, collar, and hair.

Flowers were fashioned into elaborate wreaths and garlands by the ancient Greeks. The best wreath makers were often commissioned by wealthy Greeks to make wreaths for gifts, awards, or for decoration. *Chaplets*, a special wreath for the head, were especially popular. *Cornucopia*, a horn shaped container still used today, was filled with arrangements of flowers, fruits, and vegetables. Flowers arranged into wreaths and garlands were also popular during the Roman Period and well through to the Middle Ages.

The Victorian Era saw great development in the art of floral design. There was enormous enthusiasm for flowers, plants, and gardens; the most cultured young ladies were often schooled in the art of flower arrangement. Rules were first established regarding function and design. Magazines and books about floral arrangement were also published during this time. Proper Victorian ladies often had fresh *nosegays*, or *tussie-mussies*, a hand-held arrangement of tightly knotted flowers, for sentimental reasons, if not to freshen the air. *Posy holders*, fancy carriers for these small floral arrangements, came into fashion. Some were made of ivory, glass, or mother-of-pearl, and were elaborately decorated with jewels or etchings. Flowers were also made into small arrangements and tucked into a lady's décolletage inside aptly named containers, *bosom bottles*.

Ikebana, the Japanese art of floral arrangement since the 6th century, has been a principal influence on formal flower arrangement design. Its popularity still continues today. In the 1950s, *Free Form Expression* developed, incorporating pieces of driftwood and figurines within arrangements of flowers and live plants.

Floral traditions of the past still have an impact on us today. It is still fashionable to mark special occasions with flowers, be it an anniversary, wedding, or birthday. People continue to use flowers to commemorate the dead. Today's floral arrangements reflect the current style, trends, and tastes. The best floral designers will follow the developing fashions and creatively adapt them to his or her arrangements.

The Job

From simple birthday bouquets to lavish wedding arrangements, floral designers define a sentiment, a mood, or make an impression, using flowers as their medium of expression. Along with live flowers, designers may use silk flowers or foliage, fresh fruit, twigs, or incorporate decorative items such as candles, balloons, ribbons, and stuffed animals to their arrangements. Good equipment—foam, wire, wooden or plastic picks, shears, florist's knife, tape, and a variety of containers—are essential. Techniques such as wiring flower stems, or shading the tips of blooms with paint or glitter, are often used to give floral arrangements a finished look. Familiarity with different species of flowers and plants, as well as creativity, and knowledge of elements of design is what distinguishes a good floral designer from the ordinary.

Floral designers are fortunate to have a number of employment paths from which to choose. Some designers are employed at flower shops, while some opt to work independently. Aurora Gagni, proprietress of Floral Elegance, is one such entrepreneur. A registered nurse by training, but creative by nature, Gagni always enjoyed making crafts. "I would see a picture of a flower arrangement in a magazine, and try to duplicate it, but I would always add and experiment and make it my own creation." Gagni made floral arrangements, wreaths, and displays for family, friends, and coworkers, who in turn spread word of Gagni's abilities. "At one point, I found myself giving bow-making lessons at work!" In time, she had a steady, and growing number of customers who relied on her skills.

What persuaded Gagni to give up nursing and go into business for herself? "My kids!" she answers. Indeed, this job perk is an attractive one, especially for someone juggling a career with family. Gagni conducts her business almost entirely from her home, and is available for the "many little things"— driving to and from sports events, delivering forgotten lunch boxes, and of course, homework.

Gagni tackles a variety of floral requests, but weddings are her specialty. While a typical wedding day lasts a few hours, the planning stage can take months. "Usually, the bride and groom look at my book," Gagni says, "and decide if they like my work." If so, the contract is "closed"—the contract agreement is signed, a budget is set, and a down payment is made—several months before the wedding day. Soon after, designs are made keeping the budget in mind. Many brides wish for orchids with a carnation budget. "I try to accommodate what type of flower, or color, or look the customer wants," Gagni explains, sometimes making alternate suggestions, especially if the price is an issue, or if the flower is difficult to obtain. Gagni orders necessary supplies weeks in advance and scouts for upcoming sales. She notifies her floral wholesalers in advance of any flowers that are seasonal or difficult to obtain. Also, she visits the church and reception hall to check on details such as size, location, and any restrictions. The quickest route to both destinations is also mapped out to ensure prompt delivery of the flowers.

Gagni periodically checks in with the bride about any last minute changes. Often times, more corsages or more banquet table centerpieces are needed to accommodate extra guests. Bows are tied and secured with wire about two weeks before the wedding. Three days before the wedding, flowers are picked and kept fresh in buckets of water treated with floral preservatives. The actual arranging, done in Gagni's basement, is begun the night before the wedding—bricks of floral foam, treated with water and preservatives, keep the flowers in place. Bouquets and corsages are delivered to the bride's home on the morning of the wedding; and pew ribbons, flower arrangements, and corsages for the groom's party, are brought to the church. Gagni then goes to the hall to set up for the reception. Final touch-ups are given to table centerpieces, the head table is decorated, and the last of many details are tackled.

Gagni hires additional help for large contracts, especially to assist with the final arrangements. Her children also help when needed, and her husband is her unofficial delivery driver.

Most retail floral businesses keep a relatively small staff. Sales workers help customers place their orders; they also take care of phone orders. Drivers are hired to make deliveries. Sometimes assistant designers are employed.

Requirements

High School

Take art and design classes while in high school. After all, creativity is an important buzz word in this industry. Biology classes would be helpful in learning about plants and flowers. Do you have aspirations of owning a flower establishment? Sign up for business-related courses and computer classes—they will help make you a better entrepreneur.

Postsecondary Training

In the past, floral designers learned their craft on the job, usually working as an assistant or apprentice to an experienced designer. Most designers today, however, pursue advanced education and certification. Certification is not mandatory in this industry, but it does have some pull when applying for design positions. There are numerous universities that offer degrees in floriculture and horticulture, as well as community colleges and independent schools offering certification in floral design.

Programs vary from school to school, lasting anywhere from days to years depending on the type of degree or certification. The American Floral Art School, a state approved and licensed vocational school located in Chicago, Illinois, offers certification in modern floral design, with course schedules from one to three weeks. The curriculum includes the fundamentals of artistic floral design, general instruction in picking or wiring, tinting, and arranging flowers, different types of arrangements and their containers, fashion flowers and wedding flowers, and flower shop management.

Some schools, such as the Rittners School of Floral Design, based in Boston, Massachusetts, offer classes online. They also have a special seminar emphasizing floral business skills, a must if you plan on starting your own shop.

Other Requirements

Most people don't wake up one morning and decide to become a floral designer. If you don't have a creative and artistic inclination, you're already a step behind the rest. A good floral designer enjoys and understands plants and flowers, and can visualize a creation from the very first daffodil. Are you able to work well under pressure and deadlines, and effectively deal with vendors or wholesalers? These are daily requirements of the job. Also, be prepared to greet and accommodate all types of customers, from impatient grooms to nervous brides to grieving families. A compassionate and patient personality will help you go far in this field.

Exploring

Mulling a future in floral design? Now is the best time to determine if this career is the right one for you. As a high school student without experience, it's doubtful you'll be hired as a floral designer; but working as a cashier, flower delivery person, or an assistant are great ways to break into the industry.

What about taking some classes to test your talent? Michael's, a national arts and crafts retailer, offers floral design workshops—look for similar workshops in your area. Park district programs also have design classes, especially during the holiday seasons. Such programs are relatively inexpensive—most times the fee is just enough to cover materials used in class.

Learn the industry firsthand—why not spend a day at work with a floral designer? Explain your interest to your local florist and ask if he or she would be willing to let you observe.

Employers

According to *The Detroit News*, there are over 200,000 florists employed in the floral industry in the United States. Small, independently owned flower shops are the most common employers of florists. Large, national chains, such as Teleflora and FTD, supply additional jobs. Flower departments, now a staple in larger grocery stores, also employ floral designers.

Starting Out

Some floral designers get their start by working as assistant designers. Others, especially if they are certified, may be hired as floral designers. Experienced designers may concentrate in a certain area, such as weddings, and become wedding specialists. Gagni needed to apply for a tax identification number before she officially "opened" her business. This number is necessary to establish accounts with wholesalers and greenhouses, as well as for tax purposes. It would be wise to consult with business or legal experts regarding income tax issues, promotion and advertising, and other matters dealing with operating your own business.

Professionals in floral design maintain a portfolio of their best designs. A portfolio is useful when applying for membership in floral associations, classes, and when wooing potential clients.

Advancement

Advancement in this field depends on the interest of the individual. Some floral designers are content to work at small local shops, especially if they have created a name for themselves in the area they serve. Others decide to try employment with larger national chains such as TeleFlora, or 1-800-FLOWERS. Superstore grocery chains now boast full service floral departments, creating many job opportunities for designers.

Do you possess an entrepreneurial nature? Maybe owning a floral business—home-based or established in the middle of your town's business district—is in your future. Still other options include entering the field of landscape design; interior landscaping for offices, shopping centers, and hotels; or a large floral design specialty.

Many of Gagni's contracts are wedding related so it makes sense that her business branches out accordingly. Party favors, cake toppers, and the veil and cord—elements unique in many Latin wedding ceremonies—are some items Gagni customizes for her clients.

Earnings

Experience counts for a lot when it comes to a designer's salary. According to a 1997 salary survey conducted by *Floral Finance*, designers with one year of experience averaged $6.15 an hour, with a low of $4.25 and a high of $11.00. Those with three or more years of experience earned an average hourly rate of $8.39, ranging from $5.00 to $17.00. Manager/designers averaged about $10.35 an hour (low—$5.00; high—$25.00). Geographic location plays a part in salary differences, as well. Floral designers on the East and West Coasts traditionally enjoy higher than average salaries, compared to other parts of the United States. However, this recent salary survey shows the Upper Midwest and Northwest areas had marked improvement. Stores located in large urban areas tend to have higher annual sales than those found in rural areas, resulting in higher pay for their employees.

Depending on the store, designers may be offered sick and vacation time, health and life insurance, as well as other benefits.

Work Environment

Flowers can be purchased almost anywhere, from small strip-mall flower shops to large national chains to the neighborhood grocery store. This availability means that floral designers can work almost anywhere—from remote rural areas to busy cities.

Retail floral designers can expect to have comfortable work surroundings. Most floral shops are cool, clean, and well decorated to help attract customers. Glass refrigerators filled with fresh flowers, live plants and flower arrangements, and arts and crafts are typical items in any flower shop. Work stations for making floral pieces are usually found in the back of the store, along with supplies, containers, and necessary equipment.

Expect to spend the majority of the time on your feet—either standing while working on an arrangement, consulting with customers regarding types of flowers, or on a flower buying expedition. Most retail-based designers work a normal eight-hour work day with a day off during the week. Weekends are especially busy (think weddings) and holidays notoriously so. Christmas, Mother's Day, and Valentine's Day are peak times for floral orders. Long work hours are the norm during these times to accommodate the heavy demand for flowers.

Most designers, if contracted to work a wedding, will travel to the church or the banquet hall to make sure the church arrangements or the table arrangements are properly set up.

Outlook

The future for floral designers looks bright as a daisy. The field of design, floral design included, is expected to grow faster than the average for all other occupations through 2008, according to the U.S. Department of Labor. At least one flower shop is situated in even the smallest of towns. The emergence of full service floral departments in grocery stores, as well as international floral wire services such as Amlings, FTD, and TeleFlora, contributes to job availability. Floral experts who are able to create exciting and original designs will be in high demand. Certified designers may have an edge for the best jobs.

A growing population with large disposable incomes is good news for this industry. Sending flowers to mark an occasion is an old tradition that still has impact today. However, advancement in this career is limited unless you choose to enter management or open a business. Also, starting hourly pay for floral designers is considerably lower than in other design fields.

For More Information

For education and certification information, contact:

Society of American Florists
1601 Duke Street
Alexandria, VA 22314
Tel: 703-836-8700
Web: http://www.safnow.org/

For membership information, contact:

The American Institute of Floral Designers
720 Light Street
Baltimore, MD 21230-3816
Tel: 410-752-3318
Email: aifd@assnhqtrs.com
Web: http://www.libertynet.org/flowrsho/village/AIFD.html

For information on certification and course schedules, contact:

American Floral Art School
529 South Wabash Avenue, Suite 610
Chicago, IL 60605
Tel: 312-922-9328

For information on educational opportunities, including online courses, contact:

Rittners School of Floral Design
2345 Marlborough Street
Boston, MA 02115
Tel: 617-267-3824
Email: Stevert@tiac.net
Web: http://www.tiac.net/users/stevrt/index.html

Franchise Owners

Business Mathematics	School Subjects
Following instructions Leadership/management	Personal Skills
Primarily indoors Primarily one location	Work Environment
High school diploma	Minimum Education Level
$25,000 to $87,000 to $171,000+	Salary Range
None available	Certification or Licensing
Faster than the average	Outlook

Overview

A *franchise owner* contracts with a company to sell the company's products or services. After paying an initial fee, and agreeing to pay the company a certain percentage of revenue, the franchise owner can use the company's name, logo, and guidance. McDonald's, Subway, and Dairy Queen are some of the top franchise opportunities; these companies have franchises all across the country. Franchises account for over 80 billion dollars in annual sales in the United States, and 40 percent of all U.S. retail sales.

History

Know anybody with an antique Singer sewing machine? Chances are, it was originally sold by one of the first franchise operations. During the Civil War, the Singer Sewing Machine Company recognized the cost-efficiency of franchising, and allowed dealers across the country to sell its sewing machines. Coca-Cola, as well as the Ford Motor Company and other automobile manufacturers, followed Singer's lead in the early 20th century by granting individuals the rights to sell their products. Franchising, however, didn't quite catch on until after World War II, when the needs for products and services across the country boomed, right along with the population. Ray Kroc (1902-84) jumped on the bandwagon with his McDonald's restaurants in the 1950s—the McDonald's franchise has been one of the top money-making franchise opportunities ever since.

Franchises have changed somewhat over the last 20 to 30 years. Abuses of the franchise system brought new government regulations in the 1970s, and the government has been actively involved in protecting the rights of franchisers and franchisees. Also, single-unit ownership, the "mom and pop" operations, is giving way to multiple-unit ownership. A majority of franchisees own more than one of the franchiser's units.

The Job

Get off the Subway at Hobby Town, then take the Candy Express to the Children's Orchard. No, this isn't some strange journey in a franchise fever dream—it could be any mall or main street in the United States. Experts predicted that franchises would account for more than half of all retail sales after 2000. Franchisers (those companies that sell franchise businesses) and franchisees (those who buy the businesses) are sharing in the billions of dollars that franchise businesses take in. You probably have your favorites—maybe you indulge in the occasional cruller from Krispy Kreme, or challenge your kidneys with a daily gallon of soda from the corner 7-11. If you're interested in starting your own business, you may feel more secure investing in a franchise opportunity. If you've got some money to invest, and you're prepared to devote yourself full-time to your own business, then you may be able to enjoy a part of that company's success.

There's a franchise for practically every type of product and service imaginable. In addition to the familiar McDonald's and Burger King, other franchise operations are providing opportunities: businesses that offer temporary help; maid services; weight control centers; custom picture framing; stained glass overlay. No matter what business you'd like to break into, there's probably a franchise opportunity to consider.

Depending on the size and nature of the franchise you own, your responsibilities differ. With a large initial investment, you may be able to hire managers and staff members to assist you; with a smaller business, you'll be handling most, if not all, of the job responsibilities yourself. Though you'll have some assistance from the franchiser in terms of training, marketing guidance, and established business systems, the business is essentially your own—you've paid a franchise fee, purchased equipment, and rented space. You'll be handling many administrative details, such as record-keeping, creating budgets, and preparing reports for the franchiser. You'll also be hiring employees, scheduling work hours, and preparing payroll. Using the franchiser's marketing methods, you'll advertise your business. The practices and systems of franchisers differ, so you'll need to carefully research the franchise before you buy into it.

You may be working directly with your clientele. Of course, someone who owns multiple units of the McDonald's franchise probably won't be taking orders at the counter; but someone who owns a single unit of a smaller operation, like a pool maintenance service, may be actively involved in the work at hand, and in meeting the customers.

Donna Weber of Redmond, Washington, owns a Jazzercise franchise. Jazzercise is the world's largest dance fitness franchise corporation, with over 4,700 Jazzercise-certified instructors leading workouts for 450,000 students. "I own and teach seven Jazzercise classes a week, in two different suburbs around the Seattle area," Weber says. After investing with an initial low franchise fee, Weber went through much training and testing; the training involves instruction on exercise physiology, dance/exercise technique, and safety issues, as well as instruction on the business aspect of owning a franchise. After training, Weber received certification, and started her business. She pays a monthly fee to Jazzercise, and in return receives choreography notes to new songs, and videos demonstrating the exercises.

In addition to conducting classes, Weber spends some part of every work day preparing paper work for the corporate headquarters. "And I keep track of my students' attendance and write personal postcards to those I haven't seen in a while, those who are having birthdays, those who need some personal recognition for a job well done, etc." Weber must also regularly learn new routines. "I teach three different formats," she says, "regular aerobics, step, and a circuit-training class each week, so there is a lot of prep to do a good, safe class."

Your experience with a franchise will also be affected by the name-recognition of the business. If it's a fairly new business, you may have to take on much of the responsibility of promoting it. If it is a well-established business, customers and clients already know what to expect from your operation.

Requirements

High School

Business, math, economics, and accounting courses will be the most valuable to you in preparing for franchise ownership. Before buying into a franchise, you'll have to do a lot of research into the company, and you'll be analyzing a lot of information, including local demographics, to determine whether a business is a sound investment. English and composition is important for developing communication skills in establishing relationships with franchisers and customers. Join your high school business club to meet local franchisees, and to learn about the issues affecting business owners.

Postsecondary Training

There is certain to be a franchise opportunity for you, no matter what your education background. When franchisers consider your application for the right to purchase a unit, they'll take into consideration your previous experience in the area. Obviously, a real estate company is unlikely to take a risk on you if you've never had any experience as a broker. There are some franchise opportunities that require degrees; for example, to own an environmental consulting agency, a business which helps companies meet government environmental standards, you'll have to be an engineer or geologist. But there are also many companies willing to sell to someone wanting to break into a new business. Franchisers will often include special training as part of the initial franchise fee.

Survey results published by *Franchise Times Magazine* in 1996, showed that 87 percent of franchisees have attended college or have college degrees. This reflects the fact that many franchisees have worked for many years in other professions in order to have the money and security needed for starting new businesses.

Certification or Licensing

You may have to obtain a small business license to own a franchise unit in your state. Because of the varied nature of franchise opportunities, there's no standard certification. Some franchisers, however, have their own certification process and require their franchisees to go through training.

Other Requirements

As with any small business, you need self-motivation and discipline in order to make your franchise unit successful. Though you'll have some help from your franchiser, the responsibilities of ownership are your own. You'll also need a good credit rating to be eligible for a bank loan, or you'll need enough money of your own for the initial investment. You should be a fairly cautious person—many people are taken every year in fraudulent franchise schemes. But at the same time, you should feel comfortable taking some risks.

Exploring

The International Franchise Association (IFA) hosts a very informative Web site, and publishes *Franchising World Magazine*; check out these sources for some insight into the concerns of franchisees. Also, read some of the many business magazines that report on small business opportunities. Many of these magazines, such as *Entrepreneur,* publish special editions dealing specifically with franchises.

Many of the establishments where high school students find part-time jobs are franchise units. If working for McDonald's, Subway, Dairy Queen, or one of the many other franchised restaurants, arrange to meet the owner to discuss the pros and cons of franchise ownership. Or you may want to choose the type of franchise that interests you, then go speak to a local unit owner. Also, most franchise companies will send you brochures about their franchise opportunities.

Employers

There are a number of franchise directories available that list hundreds of franchise opportunities in diverse areas. While some franchisers sell units all across the country, others only do business in a few states. Some of the most successful franchises can guarantee a franchisee great revenue, but these franchise units can require hundreds of thousands of dollars for initial investment.

Many franchisees own more than one franchise unit with a company; some even tie two different franchises together in a practice called "cross-branding." For example, you may own a pizza franchise, as well as an ice cream franchise housed in the same restaurant. Or you may own a convenience store with a fast-food outlet.

Starting Out

Before you invest a cent, or sign any papers, you should do an extensive amount of research into the franchise, particularly if it's a fairly new company. There are many disreputable franchise operations, so you need to be certain of what you're investing in. Lawyers and franchise consultants offer their services to assist people in choosing franchises; some consultants also conduct seminars. The Federal Trade Commission (FTC) publishes *The FTC Consumer Guide to Buying a Franchise* and other relevant publications. IFA also provides franchise-buying advice.

You'll need money for the initial franchise fee and for the expenses of the first few years of business. You may pursue a loan from the bank, from business associates, the Small Business Administration, or you may use your own savings. In some cases your start-up costs will be very low; in others you'll need money for a computer, rental of work space, equipment, signs, and staff. The average start-up cost for a franchise unit is $140,000, but that average includes hotels and motels. A more common cost is between $50,000 and $60,000. Some franchises can cost much less. Weber's Jazzercise franchise required an initial $600 franchise fee. Though her business has been successful, she must share her gross income. "Twenty percent of that goes back to Jazzercise each month as a fee, I pay about 23 percent of the gross for monthly rent, and 8.6 percent to the state of Washington for sales tax collected on the price of my tickets. There are lots of women grossing $75,000 a year doing this, and there are some who choose to do this for fun and make nothing in return. It's all in how you make it work for you."

Advancement

A new franchise unit usually takes a few years to turn profitable. Once your business has proven a success, you may choose to invest in other franchise units with the same company. You may also be able to afford to hire management and other staff to take on some of the many responsibilities of the business.

Earnings

Franchisers will often provide potential franchisees with information about earnings; when making these earnings claims, a franchiser is required to provide proof of them. Gallup poll results published in 1992 stated the average pretax income of franchise owners was $124,290. This figure proved to be controversial—some experts considered the figure too high. But a survey conducted by *Franchise Times Magazine* in 1997 supported the earlier findings. The survey found the median net pretax earnings to be $171,000 a year (including the salaries drawn by the franchisees). The median gross revenue figure was $447,000. Over 27 percent of the survey respondents had gross annual revenues exceeding one million dollars.

Work Environment

Owning your own franchise unit can be demanding, requiring work of 60 to 70 hours a week, but you'll have the satisfaction of knowing that the business's success is a result of your own hard work. You can buy into opportunities that are less demanding, and may only require a part-time commitment. "I'm not getting rich," Weber says, "but I love my job and I love being my own boss. I can schedule my vacations when I want; we usually don't close our classes down, we hire certified Jazzercise substitutes."

The work may be very stressful if you're handling all the details of the business yourself, and dealing with the hiring and management of a staff can also be difficult. In some situations, much of your work will be limited to an office setting; in other situations, such as with a home inspection service or a maid service, you'll be driving to remote sites to work with clients. Some franchises are mobile in nature, and will involve a lot of traveling within a designated region.

Outlook

Entrepreneur magazine makes predictions about the best franchise opportunities every year; recent trends include juice bars, senior day care, vitamin sales, and a resurgence of frozen yogurt and fitness establishments. Home-based franchises, such as Internet consulting, mystery shopping, and career coaching, are expected to increase in popularity. The success of an individual franchise unit will depend on the fads of the time, the popularity of the product or service, and the number of franchise units in your region.

While some experts say that the success rate of franchises is very high, and a great deal of money can be made with a franchise unit, others say franchising isn't as successful as starting an independent business. According to the Department of Commerce, less than 5 percent of franchised outlets have failed each year since 1971. However, when reporting figures, franchisers don't always consider a unit as failing if it is under different ownership, but still in operation.

For More Information

For general information about franchising, and to learn about specific franchise opportunities, contact:

International Franchise Association (IFA)
1350 New York Avenue, NW, Suite 900
Washington, DC 20005-4709
Tel: 202-628-8000
Email: ifa@franchise.org
Web: http://www.franchise.org

For FTC publications regarding franchising, contact:

Federal Trade Commision Board (FTC)
Public Reference Branch
Federal Trade Commission
Washington, DC 20580
Tel: 202-326-3128
Web: http://www.ftc.gov

For other information about buying a franchise, contact:

American Association of Franchisees and Dealers
PO Box 81887
San Diego, CA 92138-1887
Tel: 800-733-9858
Email: Benefits@AAFD.org
Web: http://www.aafd.org

Jewelers and Jewelry Repairers

School Subjects
Art
Technical/Shop

Personal Skills
Artistic
Mechanical/manipulative

Work Environment
Primarily indoors
Primarily one location

Minimum Education Level
High school diploma
Apprenticeship

Salary Range
$10,400 to $27,500 to $50,000+

Certification or Licensing
None available

Outlook
About as fast as the average

Overview

Jewelers fabricate, either from their own design or one by a design specialist, rings, necklaces, bracelets, and other jewelry out of gold, silver, or platinum. *Jewelry repairers* alter ring sizes, reset stones, and refashion old jewelry. Restringing beads and stones, resetting clasps and hinges, and mending breaks in ceramic and metal pieces also are aspects of jewelry repair.

A few jewelers are also *gemologists*, who examine, grade, and evaluate gems, or *gem cutters*, who cut, shape, and polish gemstones. Many jewelers also repair watches and clocks.

History

People have always worn adornments of some type. Early cave dwellers fashioned jewelry out of shells or the bones, teeth, or claws of animals. Beads have been found in the graves of prehistoric peoples. During the Iron Age, jewelry was made of ivory, wood, or metal. Precious stones were bought and sold at least 4,000 years ago in ancient Babylon, and there was widespread trade in jewelry by the Phoenicians and others in the Mediterranean and Asia Minor. The ancient Greeks and Romans were particularly fond of gold. Excavations of ancient Egyptian civilization show extremely well crafted jewelry. It was during this time, it is believed, that jewelers first combined gems with precious metals.

Many of the metals jewelers use today, such as gold, silver, copper, brass, and iron, were first discovered or used by ancient jewelers. During the Heshamite Empire, a court jeweler discovered iron while seeking a stronger metal to use in battles. During the Renaissance period in Europe, jewelers became increasingly skillful. Artists such as Botticelli and Cellini used gold and silver with precious stones of every sort to create masterpieces of the gold and silversmiths' trades. Jewelers perfected the art of enameling during this time.

Many skilled artisans brought their trades to Colonial America. The first jewelers were watchmakers, silversmiths, and coppersmiths. In early America, a versatile craft worker might create a ring or repair the copper handle on a cooking pot. By the 1890s, New York City had emerged as a center of the precious metal jewelry industry. It became a center for the diamond trade as well as for other precious stones. The first jewelry store, as we know it today, opened at the turn of the 19th century.

By the early 20th century, machines were used to create jewelry, and manufacturing plants began mass production of costume jewelry. These more affordable items quickly became popular and made jewelry available to large numbers of people.

New York City continues today as a leading center of the precious metals industry and jewelry manufacturing in the United States. Along with Paris and London, it is a prime location for many fine jewelry designers.

During the 1980s, a small niche of jewelers began creating their own designs and either making them themselves or having other jewelers fabricate them. Also called *jewelry artists*, they differ from more traditional designers both in the designs they create and the methods and materials they use. They sell their designer lines of jewelry in small boutiques, galleries, or at crafts shows or market them to larger retail stores. Many of these jewelers open their own stores. The American Jewelry Design Council was founded in 1990 to help promote designer jewelry as an art form.

The Job

Jewelers may design, make, sell, or repair jewelry. Many jewelers combine two or more of these skills. Designers conceive and sketch ideas for jewelry that they may make themselves or have made by another craftsperson. The materials of the jeweler and the jewelry repairer usually are precious and semiprecious or synthetic stones and gold, silver, and platinum. The jeweler begins by forming an article in wax or metal with carving tools; the jeweler then places the wax model in a casting ring and pours plaster into the ring to form a mold. The mold is inserted into a furnace to melt the wax and a metal model is cast from the plaster mold. The jeweler pours the precious molten metal into the mold or uses a centrifugal casting machine to cast the article. Cutting, filing, and polishing are final touches to the item.

Jewelers do most of their work sitting down. They use small hand and machine tools, such as drills, files, saws, soldering irons, and jewelers' lathes. They often wear an eye "loupe," or magnifying glass. They constantly use their hands and eyes and need good finger-hand dexterity.

Most jewelers specialize in creating or making certain kinds of jewelry or in a particular operation, such as making, polishing, or stone-setting models and tools. Specialists include gem cutters; stone setters; fancy-wire drawers; locket, ring, and hand chain makers; and sample makers.

Silversmiths design, assemble, decorate, or repair silver articles. They may specialize in one or more areas of the jewelry field such as repairing, selling, or appraising. About 19,330 individuals are employed in this field. *Jewelry engravers* carve printing, identification, or decoration on jewelry. *Watchmakers* repair, clean, and adjust mechanisms of watches and clocks.

Gem and diamond workers select, split, saw, cut, shape, polish, or drill gems and diamonds used in jewelry or for tools and industrial purposes, using measuring instruments, machines, or hand tools. Some work as diamond die polishers, while others are gem cutters. Fewer than 600 of these specialists are employed in jewelry making today. Others in the industry may perform such operations as precision casting and modeling of molds, or setting precious and semiprecious stones for jewelry. They may make gold or silver chains and cut designs or lines in jewelry using hand tools or cutting machines. Still others work as pearl restorers or jewelry bench hands.

Experienced jewelers may become qualified to make and repair any kind of jewelry. Assembly line methods are used to produce costume jewelry and some types of precious jewelry, but the models and tools needed for factory production must be made by highly skilled jewelers. Some molds and models for manufacturing are designed and created using computer-aided design/manufacturing (CAD/CAM) systems. Costume jewelry often is made by a die stamping process. In general, the more precious the metals, the less automated the manufacturing process.

Some jewelers and jewelry repairers are self-employed; others work for manufacturing and retail establishments. Workers in a manufacturing plant include skilled, semiskilled, and unskilled positions. Skilled positions include jewelers, ring makers, engravers, toolmakers, electroplaters, and stone cutters and setters. Semiskilled positions include polishers, repairers, toolsetters, and solderers. Unskilled workers are press operators, carders, and linkers.

Although some jewelers operate their own retail stores, an increasing number of jewelry stores are owned or managed by business persons who are not jewelers. In such instances, a jeweler or jewelry repairer may be employed by the owner, or the store may send its repairs to a trade shop operated by a jeweler who specializes in repair work. Jewelers who operate their own stores sell jewelry, watches, and, frequently, such merchandise as silverware, china, and glassware. Many retail jewelry stores are located in or near large cities, with the eastern section of the country providing most of the employment in jewelry manufacturing.

Other jobs in the jewelry business include *appraisers*, who examine jewelry and determine its value and quality; *sales staff*, who set up and care for jewelry displays, take inventory, and help customers; and *buyers*, who purchase jewelry, gems, and watches from wholesalers so they can resell the items to the public in retail stores.

Requirements

High School

A high school education usually is necessary for persons desiring to enter the jewelry trade. High school courses in chemistry, physics, mechanical drawing, and art are especially useful. Computer-aided design classes are helpful for those planning to design jewelry. Sculpture and metalworking classes provide training for students interested in those areas.

Postsecondary Training

A large number and variety of educational and training programs are available in jewelry and jewelry repair. Trade schools and community colleges offer a variety of programs, including classes in basic jewelry-making skills, techniques, use and care of tools and machines, stone setting, casting, polishing, and gem identification. Programs usually run from 6 to 36 months, although individual classes are shorter and can be taken without enrolling in an entire program.

Some colleges and universities offer programs in jewelry store management, metalwork, and jewelry design. You can also find classes at fashion institutes, art schools, and art museums. In addition, you can take correspondence courses and continuing education classes. For sales and managerial positions in a retail store, college experience is usually helpful. Recommended classes are sales techniques, gemology, advertising, accounting, business administration, and computers.

The work of the jeweler and jewelry repairer may also be learned through an apprenticeship or by informal on-the-job training. The latter often includes instruction in design, quality of precious stones, and chemistry of metals. The apprentice becomes a jeweler upon the successful completion of a two-year apprenticeship and passing written and oral tests covering the trade. The apprenticeship generally focuses on casting, stone setting, and engraving.

Most jobs in manufacturing require on-the-job training, although many employers prefer to hire individuals who have completed a technical education program.

Other Requirements

Jewelers and jewelry repairers need to have extreme patience and skill to handle the expensive materials of the trade. Although the physically disabled may find employment in this field, superior eye-hand coordination is essential. Basic mechanical skills such as filing, sawing, and drilling are vital to the jewelry repairer. Jewelers who work from their own designs need creative and artistic ability. They also should have a strong understanding of metals and their properties. Retail jewelers and those who operate or own trade shops and manufacturing establishments must work well with people and have a knowledge of merchandising and business management and practices. Sales staff should be knowledgeable and friendly, and buyers must have good judgment, self-confidence, and leadership abilities. Because of the expensive nature of jewelry, some people working in the retail industry are bonded, which means they must pass the requirements for an insurance company to underwrite them.

Exploring

Students interested in becoming jewelers or jewelry repairers can engage in arts and crafts activities and take classes in crafts and jewelry making. Many community education programs are available through high schools, park districts, or local art stores and museums. Hobbies such as metalworking and sculpture are useful in becoming familiar with metals and the tools jewelers use. Visits to museums and fine jewelry stores to see collections of jewelry can be helpful.

If you are interested in a career in the retail field, you may work in a retail jewelry store part-time or during the summer. A job in sales, or even as a clerk, can provide a firsthand introduction to the business. You will become familiar with a jewelry store's operations, its customers, and the jewelry sold. In addition, you will learn the terminology unique to the jewelry field. Working in a retail store with an in-house jeweler or jewelry repairer provides many opportunities to observe and speak with a professional engaged in this trade. In a summer or part-time job as a bench worker or assembly line worker in a factory, you may perform only a few of the operations involved in making jewelry, but you will be exposed to many of the skills used within a manufacturing plant.

You also may want to visit retail stores and shops where jewelry is made and repaired or visit a jewelry factory. Some boutiques and galleries are owned and operated by jewelers who enjoy the opportunity to talk to people about their trade. Art fairs and craft shows where jewelers exhibit and sell their products provide a more relaxed environment where jewelers are likely to have time to discuss their work.

Employers

Jewelers are employed in a variety of settings, from production work in multinational corporations or smaller firms to jewelry stores and repair shops. Some jewelers specialize in gem and diamond work, watchmaking, jewelry appraisal, repair, or engraving where they may work in manufacturing or at the retail level. Others open their own shops, where they sell and repair jewelry and watches and in some cases, design and create jewelry.

Starting Out

A summer or part-time job in a jewelry store or the jewelry department of a department store will help you learn about the business. Another method of entering this line of work is to obtain employment in jewelry manufacturing establishments in major production centers. A trainee can acquire the many skills needed in the jewelry trade. The number of trainees accepted in this manner, however, is relatively small. Students who have completed a training program improve their chances of finding work as an apprentice or trainee. Students may learn about available jobs and apprenticeships through the placement offices of training schools they attend, from local jewelers, or from the personnel offices of manufacturing plants.

Those desiring to establish their own retail businesses find it helpful to first obtain employment with an established jeweler or a manufacturing plant. Considerable financial investment is required to open a retail jewelry store, and jewelers in such establishments find it to their advantage to be able to do repair work on watches as well as the usual jeweler's work. Less financial investment is needed to open a trade shop. These shops generally tend to be more successful in or near areas with large populations where they can take advantage of the large volume of jewelry business. Both retail jewelry stores and trade shops are required to meet local and state business laws and regulations.

Advancement

There are many opportunities for advancement in the jewelry field. Jewelers and jewelry repairers can go into business for themselves once they have mastered the skills of their trade. They may create their own designer lines of jewelry that they market and sell, or they can open a trade shop or retail store. Many self-employed jewelers gain immense satisfaction from the opportunity to specialize in one aspect of jewelry or to experiment with new methods and materials.

Workers in jewelry manufacturing have fewer opportunities for advancement than in other areas of jewelry because of the declining number of workers needed. Plant workers in semiskilled and unskilled positions can advance based on the speed and quality of their work and by perseverance. On-the-job training can provide opportunities for higher-skilled positions. Workers in manufacturing who show proficiency can advance to supervisory and management positions, or they may leave manufacturing and go to work in a retail shop or trade shop.

The most usual avenue of advancement is from employee in a factory, shop, or store to owner or manager of a trade shop or retail store. Sales is an excellent starting place for people who want to own their own store. Sales staff receive firsthand training in customer relations as well as knowledge of the different aspects of jewelry store merchandising. Sales staff may become gem experts who are qualified to manage a store, and managers may expand their territory from one store to managing several stores in a district or region. Top management in retail offers many interesting and rewarding positions to people who are knowledgeable, responsible, and ambitious. Buyers may advance by dealing exclusively with fine gems that are more expensive, and some buyers become *diamond merchants*, buying diamonds on the international market.

Jewelry designers' success depends not only on the skill with which they make jewelry but also on the ability to create new designs and to keep in touch with current trends in the consumer market. Jewelry designers attend craft shows, trade shows, and jewelry exhibitions to see what others are making and to get ideas for new lines of jewelry.

Earnings

Jewelers and silversmiths combined had a mean annual wage of about $23,820 in 1998. Starting salaries for beginning retailers and those with only a few years of experience was much less. The average annual salary for retail jewelry repairers was around $25,000. Retail sales staff earned from $5 to $7 an hour, with some workers earning a commission on what they sold. Jewelers and other workers in manufacturing had average annual salaries of $14,500 to $32,000, with jewelers making significantly more than those in unskilled or semiskilled positions. Retail store owners and jewelry artists and designers can earn anywhere from $25,000 to $50,000 or more yearly, based on their volume of business.

The 1997 mean annual income for all precision etchers and engravers was $22,660. Watchmakers earned mean annual wages of $26,700. Gem and diamond workers' annual income was $25,290. Most employers offer benefit packages that include paid holidays and vacations and health insurance. Retail stores may offer discounts on store purchases.

Work Environment

Jewelers work in a variety of environments. Some self-employed jewelers design and create jewelry in their homes; others work in small studios or trade shops. Some use computer-aided designing software to create their sketches. Jewelers who create their own designer lines of jewelry may travel to retail stores and other sites to promote their merchandise. Many designers also attend trade shows and exhibitions to learn more about current trends. Some sell their jewelry at both indoor and outdoor art shows and craft fairs. These shows are held on weekends, evenings, or during the week. Many jewelry artists live and work near tourist areas or in art communities.

Workers in jewelry manufacturing plants usually work in clean, air-conditioned, and relatively quiet environments. Workers in departments such as polishing, electroplating, and lacquer spraying may be exposed to fumes from chemicals and solvents. Workers may do bench work where they sit at a workstation or on an assembly line where they may be standing or sitting. Assembly line workers may operate machinery. Many workers in a manufacturing plant perform only one or two types of operations so the work can become repetitious. Most employees in a manufacturing plant work 35-hour workweeks, with an occasional need for overtime.

Retail store owners, managers, jewelers, and sales staff work a variety of hours and shifts that include weekends, especially during the Christmas season, the busiest time of year. Buyers may work more than 40 hours a week because they must travel to see wholesalers. Work settings vary from small shops and boutiques to large department stores. Most jewelry stores are clean, quiet, pleasant, and attractive. However, most jewelry store employees spend many hours on their feet dealing with customers, and buyers travel a great deal.

Outlook

In 1998, about 30,000 jewelers were employed in the United States, and about one-third of them were self-employed. The majority of the self-employed jewelers own their own stores or repair shops or specialize in designing and creating custom jewelry. Opportunities in manufacturing centers declined significantly during the 1990s as many factories closed or moved to foreign locations. Opportunities in retail were slowed slightly during the early part of the 1990s due to the growth of imported goods and a recession that slowed consumer purchasing. In the mid-1990s, though, retail stores recovered from this slump, and more opportunities became available. One-half of all salaried jewelers worked in retail establishments in 1998 and one-third were employed in manufacturing plants, according to the *Occupational Outlook Handbook*. Demand in retail is growing for people who are skilled in personnel, management, sales and promotion, advertising, floor and window display, and buying. Some jewelers work as appraisers and some stores employ an appraiser to do only that work. In most cases, though, appraisals are done by store owners or jewelers who have years of experience.

Employment of jewelers is expected to decline slightly through 2008, according to the *Occupational Outlook Handbook*. Consumers now are purchasing jewelry from mass marketers, discount stores, catalogs, television shopping shows, and the Internet as well as from traditional retail stores. This may result in some stores closing or in limited opportunities within them for employment. Jewelers and jewelry repairers will continue to be needed to replace those workers who leave the workforce or move to new positions within it. Although the number of workers in manufacturing plants is declining, opportunities in retail and as self-employed jewelers should remain steady or improve slightly.

For More Information

For a list of accredited technical schools with jewelry design programs, contact:

Accrediting Commission of Career Schools and Colleges of Technology
2101 Wilson Boulevard, Suite 302
Arlington, VA 22201

For an information packet with tuition prices, application procedures, and course descriptions, contact:

Gemological Institute of America
The Robert Mouawad Campus
5345 Armada Drive
Carlsbad, CA 92008-9525
Tel: 800-421-7250, ext. 4001

For a school directory and a copy of Careers in Retail Jewelry: A Jewelers of America Guide, *contact:*

Jewelers of America
1185 6th Avenue, 30th Floor
New York, NY 10036
Tel: 800-223-0673
Web: http://www.http://www.jewelers.org/home.html

For career and school information, contact:

Manufacturing Jewelers and Silversmiths of America
45 Royal Little Drive
Providence, RI 02904
Tel: 800-444-MJSA
Web: http://mjsa.polygon.net

Merchandise Displayers

Art Theater/Dance Technical/Shop	School Subjects
Artistic Mechanical/manipulative	Personal Skills
Primarily one location	Primarily indoors
High school diploma	Minimum Education Level
$12,000 to $23,400 to $30,000+	Salary Range
None available	Certification or Licensing
About as fast as the average	Outlook

Overview

Merchandise displayers design and install displays of clothing, accessories, furniture, and other products in windows and showcases, and on the sales floors of retail stores to attract potential customers. Display workers who specialize in dressing mannequins are known as *model dressers*. These workers use their artistic flair and imagination to create excitement and customer interest in the store. They also work with other types of merchandising to develop exciting images, product campaigns, and shopping concepts.

History

Eye-catching displays of merchandise attract customers and encourage them to buy. This form of advertising has been used throughout history. Farmers in the past who displayed their produce at markets were careful to place their largest, most unblemished, most tempting fruits and vegetables at the top of the baskets. Peddlers opened their bags and cases and arranged their wares in attractive patterns. Store owners decorated their windows with collections of articles they hoped to sell. Their business success often was a matter of chance, however, and depended heavily on their own persuasiveness and sales ability.

As glass windows became less expensive, storefronts were able to accommodate larger window frames. This exposed more of the store to passersby, and stores soon found that decorative window displays were effective in attracting customers. Today a customer may see nearly the entire store and the displays of the products it sells just by looking in the front window.

The advent of self-service stores has minimized the importance of the salesperson's personal touch. The merchandise now has to sell itself. Displays have become an important inducement for customers to buy. Advertising will bring people into stores, but an appealing product display can make the difference between a customer who merely browses and one who buys.

Merchandise displayers are needed year-round, but during the Christmas season they often execute their most elaborate work. Small retail stores generally depend on the owner or manager to create the merchandise displays, or they may hire a freelance window dresser on a part-time basis. Large retail operations, such as department stores, retain a permanent staff of display and visual merchandising specialists. Competition among these stores is intense, and their success depends on capturing a significant portion of the market. Therefore, they allocate a large share of their publicity budget to creating unique, captivating displays.

The Job

Using their imagination and creative ability, as well as their knowledge of color harmony, composition, and other fundamentals of art and interior design, merchandise displayers in retail establishments create an idea for a setting designed to show off merchandise and attract customers' attention. Often the display is planned around a theme or concept. After the display manager approves the design or idea, the display workers create the display by constructing backdrops, using hammers, saws, spray guns, and other hand tools, installing background settings, such as carpeting, wallpaper, and lighting; gathering props and other accessories; arranging mannequins and merchandise; and placing price tags and descriptive signs where they are needed.

They may be assisted in some of these tasks by carpenters, painters, or store maintenance workers. They may use merchandise from various departments of the store or props from previous displays. Sometimes they borrow special items that their business doesn't carry from other stores; for example, toys or sports equipment,. The displays are dismantled and new ones installed every few weeks. In very large stores that employ many display workers, one may specialize in carpentry, painting, making signs, or setting up interior or window displays. A *display director* usually supervises and coordinates the display workers' activities and confers with other managers to select merchandise to be featured.

Ambitious and talented display workers have many possible career avenues. The importance of visual merchandising is being recognized more and more as retail establishments compete for consumer dollars. Some display workers can advance to display director or even a position in store planning.

In addition to traditional stores, the skills of *visual marketing workers* are now in demand in many other types of establishments. Restaurants often try to present a distinct image to enhance the dining experience. Outlet stores, discount malls, and entertainment centers also use visual marketing to establish their identities with the public. Chain stores often need to make changes in or redesign all their stores and turn to display professionals for their expertise. Consumer product manufacturers also are heavily involved in visual marketing. They hire display and design workers to come up with exciting concepts, such as "in-store shops," which present a unified image of the manufacturer's products and are sold as complete units to retail stores.

There are also opportunities for employment with store fixture manufacturers. Many companies build and sell specialized props, banners, signs, displays, and mannequins and hire display workers as sales representatives to promote their products. The display workers' understanding of retail needs and their insight into the visual merchandising industry make them valuable consultants.

Commercial decorators prepare and install displays and decorations for trade and industrial shows, exhibitions, festivals, and other special events. Working from blueprints, drawings, and floor plans, they use woodworking power tools to construct installations (usually referred to as booths, no matter what their size), at exhibition halls and convention centers. They install carpeting, drapes, and other decorations, such as flags, banners, and lights. They arrange furniture and accessories to attract the people attending the exhibition. Special event producers, coordinators, and party planners may also seek out the skills of display professionals.

This occupation appeals to imaginative, artistic persons who find it rewarding to use their creative abilities to visualize a design concept and transform it into reality. Original, creative displays grow out of an awareness of current design trends and popular themes. Although display workers use inanimate objects such as props and materials, an understanding of human motivations helps them create displays with strong customer appeal.

Requirements

High School

Display workers must have at least a high school degree. Important high school subjects include art, woodworking, mechanical drawing, and merchandising. Some employers require college courses in art, interior decorating, fashion design, advertising, or related subjects.

Postsecondary Training

High schools and community and junior colleges that offer distributive education and marketing programs often include display work in the curriculum. Fashion merchandising schools and fine arts institutes also offer courses useful to display workers.

Much of the training for display workers is gained on the job. They generally start as helpers for routine tasks, such as carrying props and dismantling sets. Gradually they are permitted to build simple props and work up to constructing more difficult displays. As they become more experienced, display workers who show artistic talent may be assigned to plan simple designs. The total training time varies depending on the beginner's ability and the variety and complexity of the displays.

Other Requirements

Among the personal qualifications needed by display workers are creative ability, manual dexterity, and mechanical aptitude. Display workers should possess the strength and physical ability needed to be able to carry equipment and climb ladders. They also need agility to work in close quarters without upsetting the props.

Exploring

Display work is included in many of the marketing programs taught in high school and in community and junior colleges. Fashion merchandising schools and fine arts institutes offer courses useful for this occupation. These courses usually combine hands-on activities with the study of fashion and merchandising.

Part-time and summer jobs in department stores and other retail stores or at exhibition centers provide interested students with an overview of the display operations in these establishments. Photographers and theater groups need helpers to work with props and sets, although some may require previous experience or knowledge related to their work. Students active in school drama and photo clubs may be able to help with design. Interested persons also can read periodicals, such as *Display and Design Ideas* (http://www.ddimagazine.com/), that publish articles on the field or related subjects.

Employers

About 30,000 display workers are employed in the United States. Most of them work in department and clothing stores, but many are employed in other types of retail stores, such as variety, drug, and shoe stores. Some have their own design businesses, and some are employed by design firms that handle interior and professional window dressing for small stores. Employment of display workers is distributed throughout the country, with most of the jobs concentrated in large towns and cities.

Starting Out

School placement offices may have job listings for display workers or related positions. Persons wishing to become display workers can apply directly to retail stores, decorating firms, or exhibition centers. Openings also may be listed in the classified ads of newspapers.

A number of experienced merchandise displayers choose to work as freelance designers. Competition in this area, however, is intense, and it takes time to establish a reputation, build a list of clients, and earn an adequate income. Freelancing part time while holding down another job provides a more secure income for many display workers. Freelancing also provides beginners with opportunities to develop a portfolio of photographs of their best designs, which they can then use to sell their services to other stores.

Advancement

Display workers with supervisory ability can become regional managers. Further advancement may lead to a display director position of a large store and then head of store planning.

Another way to advance is by starting a freelance design business. This can be done with very little financial investment, although freelance design workers must spend many long hours generating new business and establishing their names in the field.

Experienced display workers also may be able to transfer their skills to jobs in other art-related fields, such as interior design or photography. These, however, require additional training.

Earnings

According to the *Occupational Outlook Handbook,* merchandise displayers averaged about $18,180 in 1998. The lowest 10 percent earned $12,680 or less; the top 10 percent earned over $28,910. Freelancers may earn as much as $30,000 a year, but their income depends entirely on their talent, reputation, number of clients, and amount of time they work.

Work Environment

Display workers usually work 35 to 40 hours a week, except during busy seasons, such as Christmas. Selling promotions and increased sales drives during targeted seasons can require the display staff to work extra hours in the evening and on weekends.

The work of constructing and installing displays requires prolonged standing, bending, stooping, and working in awkward positions. There is some risk of falling off ladders or being injured from handling sharp materials or tools, but serious injuries are uncommon.

Outlook

The employment of display workers is expected to keep pace with the average for all occupations through 2008. Growth in this profession is expected due to an expanding retail sector and the increasing popularity of visual merchandising. Most openings will occur as older, experienced workers retire or leave the occupation.

Fluctuations of the economy affect the volume of retail sales because people are less likely to spend money during recessionary times. For display workers this can result in layoffs or hiring freezes.

For More Information

This organization offers an information packet including student membership, schools with student chapters, the **Interior Design Career Guide,** *information about ASID scholarships, and a list of career specialties.*

American Society of Interior Designers (ASID)
Bonnie Cambron, Education Programs Marketing Manager
608 Massachusetts Avenue, NE
Washington, DC 20002
Tel: 202-546-34380

Student memberships in this organization provide entry to visual displays trade shows around the country, resume referral services for jobs, and scholarships for students.

National Association of Display Industries
Edwin Cossitt, Executive Director
234 Fifth Avenue, Suite 407
New York, NY 10001
Tel: 212-725-4490
Web: http://www.nadi.org

For a list of scholarships for students in visual merchandising and store design, internship programs, and a list of colleges that offer courses in visual merchandising, contact:

Planning and Visual Partnership Education
3368A Oxford Avenue
St. Louis, MO 63143
Tel: 314-645-0701

Personal Shoppers

Business
Family and Consumer Science
─────School Subjects

Following instructions
Helping/teaching
─────Personal Skills

Primarily indoors
Primarily multiple locations
─────Work Environment

High school diploma
─────Minimum Education Level

$10,000 to $22,000 to $38,000
─────Salary Range

None available
─────Certification or Licensing

Faster than the average
─────Outlook

Overview

People who don't have the time or the ability to go shopping for clothes, gifts, groceries, and other items use the services of *personal shoppers*. Personal shoppers shop department stores, look at catalogs, and surf the Internet for the best buys and most appropriate items for their clients. Relying on a sense of style and an ability to spot a bargain, a personal shopper helps clients develop a wardrobe and find gifts for friends, relatives, and employees. Though personal shoppers work all across the country, their services are in most demand in large, metropolitan areas.

History

For decades, American retailers have been working to create easier ways to shop. Mail-order was an early innovation—catalog companies like Montgomery Wards and Sears and Roebuck started business in the late 19th century to meet the shopping needs of people living in rural areas and small towns. Many consumers relied on mail-order for everything from suits and dresses to furniture and stoves; Sears even sold automobiles through the mail. Shopping for food, clothes, and gifts was considered a household chore, a responsibility that belonged to women. By the late 1800s, shopping had developed into a popular past-time in metropolitan areas. Wealthy women of leisure turned downtown shopping districts into the busiest sections of their cities, as department stores, boutiques, tea shops, and cafes evolved to serve them.

As more women joined the work force after World War II, retailers worked to make their shopping areas more convenient. Supermarkets, shopping centers, and malls became popular. Toward the end of the 20th century, shoppers began looking for even more simplicity and convenience. In the 1990s, many companies began to market their products via the Internet. In addition to Internet commerce, overworked men and women are turning to personal shoppers, professional organizers, and personal assistants to fulfill their shopping needs.

The Job

Looking for a job where you get to shop all the time, tell people what to wear, and spend somebody else's money? Though this may seem to describe the life of the personal shopper, it's not quite accurate. For one thing, you don't get to shop all the time—you will be spending some time in stores and browsing catalogs, but you're often looking for something very specific, and working as quickly as you can. And you're not so much telling people what to wear, as teaching them how to best match outfits, what colors suit them, and what styles are most appropriate for their workplaces. And, yes, you're spending someone else's money, but it's all for someone else's closet.

So, if you're not too disillusioned, read on: working as a personal shopper may still be right for you. As a personal shopper, you help people who are unable or uninterested in doing their own shopping. You'll be hired to look for that perfect gift for a difficult-to-please aunt. You'll be hired by senior citizens, or people with disabilities, to do their grocery shopping and run other shopping errands. You'll help professionals create a nice, complete wardrobe. All the while, you'll rely on your knowledge of the local marketplace in order to do the shopping quickly and efficiently.

Some personal shoppers use their backgrounds in other areas to assist clients. Someone with a background in real estate may serve as a personal shopper for houses, working for a buyer rather than a seller. These house shoppers inspect houses and do some of the client's bargaining. Those with a background in cosmetology may work as *image consultants*, advising clients on their hair, clothes, and make-up. Another shopper may have some experience in dealing antiques, and will help clients locate particular items. An interior decorator may shop for furniture and art to decorate a home.

If you're offering wardrobe consultation, you'll need to visit the client's home and evaluate his or her clothes. You'll help your clients determine what additional clothes and accessories they'll need, and you'll advise them on what jackets to wear with what pants, what skirt to wear with what blouse. Together with the client, you'll determine what additional clothes are needed to complete the wardrobe, and you'll come up with a budget. Then it's off to the stores.

Irene Kato owns I Kan Do It, a personal shopping service. She offers a variety of services, including at-home wardrobe consultation, closet organization, and gift-shopping. "Most of my shopping so far has been for clothes," Kato says. "I have a fairly good idea of what I'm looking for so I don't spend too much time in any one store if I don't see what I want right away. I can usually find two or three choices for my client and rarely have to shop another day." Kato spends about two to three hours every other day shopping, and spends about two hours a day in her office working on publicity, her budget, and corresponding with clients. Shopping for one client can take about three hours. "I have always enjoyed shopping," Kato says, "and especially like finding bargains. Waiting in lines, crowds, etc., does not bother me."

As a personal shopper, you'll likely cater to professionals needing business attire and wardrobe consultation. A smaller part of your business will be shopping for gifts. You may even supplement your business by running non-shopping errands, such as purchasing theater tickets, making deliveries, and going to the post office. Many personal shoppers also work as *professional organizers*: they go into homes and offices to organize desks, kitchens, and closets.

In addition to the actual shopping, you'll have administrative responsibilities. You'll do record-keeping, make phone calls, and schedule appointments. Self-promotion will be very important; because personal shopping is a fairly new endeavor, you have the added burden of educating the public about the service. "A personal shopper has no commodity to sell," Kato says, "only themselves. So it is twice as hard to attract clients." To publicize her business, Kato maintains a Web site that lists the services she provides and testimonials from clients. She also belongs to two professional organizations that help her network and develop her business: Executive Women International (EWI) and Giving Referrals to Other Women (GROW).

Requirements

High School

Take classes in home economics to develop budget and consumer skills, as well as learn about fashion and home design. If the class offers a sewing unit, you'll learn about tailoring, and can develop an eye for clothes sizes. Math, business, and accounting courses will prepare you for the administrative details of the job. English composition and speech classes will help you develop the communication skills you'll need for promoting your business, and for advising clients about their wardrobes.

Postsecondary Training

Many people working as personal shoppers have had experience in other areas of business. They've worked as managers in corporations or have worked as salespeople in retail stores. But because of the entrepreneurial nature of the career, you don't need any specific kind of education or training. A small-business course at your local community college, along with classes in design, fashion, and consumer science, can help you develop the skills you'll need for the job. If you're unfamiliar with the computer, you should take some classes to learn desktop publishing programs for creating business cards and other publicity material.

Other Requirements

"I seem to have an empathy for people," Kato says. "After talking with a client I know what they want and what they're looking for. I am a very good listener." In addition to these people skills, a personal shopper should be patient, and capable of dealing with the long lines and customer service of department stores. You should be creative, and able to come up with a variety of gift ideas. A sense of style is important, along with knowledge of the latest brands and designers. You'll need a good eye for colors and fabrics. You should also be well-dressed and organized so that your client will know to trust your wardrobe suggestions.

Exploring

If you've spent any time at the mall, you probably already have enough shopping experience. And if you've had to buy clothes and gifts with limited funds, then you know something about budgeting. Sign up for the services of a personal shopper in a department store; in most stores the service is free, and you'll get a sense of how a shopper works. Pay close attention to the information they request from you in the beginning, then ask them later about their decision-making process. Kato advises future personal shoppers to work a few years at a retail clothing store. "This way," she says, "you can observe the way people dress, what shapes and sizes we all are, how fashion trends come and go, and what stays."

Employers

Most of your clients will be professional men and women with high incomes and busy schedules. You'll be working with people with new jobs requiring dress clothes, but also with people who need to perk up an old wardrobe. You may work for executives in corporations who need to buy gifts for large staffs of employees. Some of your clients may be elderly or have disabilities and have problems getting out to do their shopping.

Starting Out

The start-up costs can be very low; you may only have to invest in a computer, business cards, and a reliable form of transportation. But it could take you a very long time to develop a regular clientele. You'll want to develop the business part-time while still working full-time at another, more reliable job. Some of your first clients may come from your workplace—offer free introductory services to a few people and encourage them to spread the word around and hand out your business card. You'll also need to become very familiar with the local retail establishments and the discount stores with low-cost, high-quality merchandise.

"My friends and colleagues at work," Kato says, "were always complimentary on what I wore and would ask where I bought my clothes, where they could find certain items, where were the best sales." Kato was taking the part-time approach to developing her personal shopping service, when downsizing at her company thrust her into the new business earlier than she'd planned. She had the opportunity to take an entrepreneur class at a local private university which helped her devise a business plan and taught her about the pros and cons of starting a business.

Advancement

The first few years of your personal shopper business will likely be lean. After a few years of working part-time, you may be able to turn it into a well-paying, full-time job for yourself. As more people learn about your business, you'll take on more clients. Eventually, you may be able to hire an assistant to help you with the administrative work, such as client billing and scheduling.

Earnings

Personal shoppers bill their clients in different ways: you'll set a regular fee for services, charge a percentage of the sale, or charge an hourly rate. You might use all these methods in your business; your billing method may depend on the client and the service. For example, when offering wardrobe consultation and shopping for clothes, you may find it best to charge by the hour; when shopping for a small gift, it may be more reasonable to only charge a percentage. Personal shoppers charge anywhere from $25 to $125 an hour; the average hourly rate is about $75. Successful shoppers living in a large city can make between $1,500 and $3,000 a month.

Work Environment

You'll have all the advantages of owning your own business, including setting your own hours, and keeping a flexible schedule. But you'll also have all the disadvantages, such as job insecurity and lack of benefits. "I have a bad habit of thinking about my business almost constantly," Kato says. Though you won't have to deal with the stress of a full-time office job, you will have the stress of finding new clients and keeping the business afloat entirely by yourself.

Your office will be in your home, but you'll be spending a lot of time with people, from clients to salespeople. You'll obviously spend some time in department stores; if you like to shop, this can be enjoyable even when you're not buying anything for yourself. In some cases, you'll be visiting client's homes to advise them on their wardrobe. You can expect to do a lot of traveling, driving to a department store after a meeting with a client, then back to the client with the goods.

Outlook

Personal shopping is a new business development, so anyone embarking on the career will be taking some serious risks. There's not a lot of research available about the career, no national professional organization specifically serving personal shoppers, and no real sense of the career's future. The success of Internet commerce will probably have a big effect on the future of personal shopping. If purchasing items through the Internet becomes more commonplace, personal shoppers may have to establish places for themselves on the World Wide Web. Some personal shoppers currently with Web sites offer consultation via email and help people purchase products online.

It may be in your best interest to offer as expansive a service as you can. Professional organizing is being recognized as one of the top home businesses for the future; the membership for the National Association of Professional Organizers (NAPO) has doubled every year since 1985. *Personal assistants*, those who run errands for others, have also caught the attention of industry experts, and there are programs to help you get started as an assistant.

For More Information

To learn about the career of professional organizer, contact:

National Association of Professional Organizers
P O Box 140647
Austin TX 78714
Tel: 512-206-0151
Web: http://www.napo.net

To learn about a program that can help you establish a business as a personal assistant, contact:

Personal Assistants International
1800 30th Street, Suite 220C
Boulder, CO 80301
Tel: 303-443-7646

Purchasing Agents

—School Subjects
Business
Economics
Mathematics

—Personal Skills
Helping/teaching
Technical/scientific

—Work Environment
Primarily indoors
Primarily one location

—Minimum Education Level
High school diploma

—Salary Range
$23,960 to $38,040 to $74,050+

—Certification or Licensing
Voluntary

—Outlook
Little change or more slowly than
the average

Overview

Purchasing agents work for businesses and other large organizations, such as hospitals, universities, and government agencies. They buy raw materials, machinery, supplies, and services required for the organization. They must consider cost, quality, quantity, and time of delivery.

History

Careers in the field of purchasing are relatively new and have come into real importance only in the last half of the 20th century. The first purchasing jobs emerged during the Industrial Revolution, when manufacturing plants and businesses became bigger. This led to the division of management jobs into various specialties, one of which was buying.

By the late 1800s buying was considered a separate job in large businesses. Purchasing jobs were especially important in such industries as railroads, automobiles, and steel. The trend toward creating specialized buying jobs was reflected in the founding of professional organizations, such as the National Association of Purchasing Agents (now the National Association of Purchasing Management) and the American Purchasing Society. It was not until after World War II, however, with the expansion of the U.S. government and the increased complexity of business practices, that the job of purchasing agent became firmly established.

The Job

Purchasing agents generally work for organizations that buy at least $100,000 worth of goods a year. Their primary goal is to purchase the best quality materials for the best price. To do this, the agent must consider the exact specifications for the required items, cost, quantity discounts, freight handling or other transportation costs, and delivery time. In the past, much of this information was obtained by comparing listings in catalogs and trade journals, interviewing suppliers' representatives, keeping up with current market trends, examining sample goods, and observing demonstrations of equipment. Increasingly, information can be found through computer databases. Sometimes agents visit plants of company suppliers. The agent is responsible for following up on orders and ensuring that goods meet the order specifications.

Most purchasing agents work in firms that have fewer than five employees in the purchasing department. In some small organizations, there is only one person responsible for making purchases. Very large firms, however, may employ as many as a hundred purchasing agents, each responsible for specific types of goods. In such organizations there is usually a *purchasing director* or *purchasing manager*.

Some purchasing agents seek the advice of *purchase-price analysts*, who compile and analyze statistical data about the manufacture and cost of products. Based on this information, they can make recommendations to purchasing personnel regarding the feasibility of producing or buying certain products and suggest ways to reduce costs.

Purchasing agents often specialize in a particular product or field. For example, *procurement engineers* specialize in aircraft equipment. They establish specifications and requirements for construction, performance, and testing of equipment.

Field contractors negotiate with farmers to grow or purchase fruits, vegetables, or other crops. These agents may advise growers on methods, acreage, and supplies and arrange for financing, transportation, or labor recruitment.

Head tobacco buyers are engaged in the purchase of tobacco on the auction warehouse floor. They advise other buyers about grades and quantities of tobacco and suggest prices.

Grain buyers manage grain elevators. They are responsible for evaluating and buying grain for resale and milling. They are concerned with the quality, market value, shipping, and storing of grain.

Grain broker-and-market operators buy and sell grain for investors through the commodities exchange. Like other brokers, they work on a commission basis.

Requirements

High School

Most purchasing and buying positions require at least a bachelor's degree. Helpful high school subjects are English, mathematics, social science, and economics.

Postsecondary Training

Although it is possible to obtain an entry-level purchasing job with only a high school degree, many employers prefer to hire college graduates, and some require college degrees. College work should include courses in general economics, purchasing, accounting, statistics, and business management. A familiarity with computers also is desirable. Some colleges and universities offer majors in purchasing.

Purchasing agents with a master's degree in business administration, engineering, technology, or finance tend to have the best jobs and highest salaries. Companies that manufacture machinery or chemicals may require a degree in engineering or a related field. A civil service examination is required for employment in government purchasing positions.

Certification or Licensing

There are no specific licenses or certification requirements imposed by law for purchasing agents. There are, however, several professional organizations to which many purchasing agents belong, including the National Association of Purchasing Management, the National Institute of Government Purchasing, and the American Purchasing Society. These organizations confer certification on applicants who meet their educational and other requirements and who pass the necessary examinations. The American Purchasing Society, for example, offers two types of certification, the certified purchasing professional (CPP) and certified purchasing executive (CPE). Although such certification is not essential, it is a recognized mark of professional competence that enhances a purchasing agent's opportunities for promotion to top management positions.

Other Requirements

Purchasing agents should have calm temperaments and the self-confidence to be firm in decision making. Because they work with other people, they need to be diplomatic, tactful, and cooperative. A thorough knowledge of business practices and understanding of the needs and activities of the employer are essential. It also is helpful to be familiar with social and economic changes in order to predict the amounts or types of products to buy.

Exploring

If you are interested in becoming a purchasing agent, you can learn more about the field through a summer job in the purchasing department of a business. Even working as a stock clerk can offer some insight into the job of purchasing agent or buyer. You may also talk with experienced purchasing agents about the job and read periodicals, such as *Purchasing* magazine (http://www.manufacturing.net/magazine/purchasing/), that publish articles on the field. Keeping abreast of economic trends, fashion styles, or other indicators may help you to predict the market for particular products, and making educated and informed predictions is a basic part of any buying job.

Employers

Purchasing agents and buyers work for a wide variety of businesses, both wholesale and retail, as well as for government agencies. Employers range from small stores, where buying may be only one function of a manager's job, to multinational corporations, where a buyer may specialize in one type of item and buy in enormous quantity. Nearly every business that sells products requires someone to purchase the goods to be sold. These businesses are located nearly everywhere there is a community of people, from small towns to large cities. Of course, the larger the town, the more businesses and thus more buying positions. Larger cities provide the best opportunities for higher salaries and advancement.

Starting Out

Students without a college degree may be able to enter the field as clerical workers and then receive on-the-job training in purchasing. A college degree, though, is required for most higher positions. College and university placement services offer assistance to graduating students in locating jobs.

Entry into the purchasing department of a private business can be made by direct application to the company. Some purchasing agents start in another department, such as accounting, shipping, or receiving, and transfer to purchasing when an opportunity arises. Many large companies send newly hired agents through orientation programs, where they learn about goods and services, suppliers, and purchasing methods.

Another means of entering the field is through the military. Service in the Quartermaster Corps of the Army or the procurement divisions of the Navy or Air Force can provide excellent preparation either for a civilian job or a career position in the service.

Advancement

In general, purchasing agents begin by becoming familiar with departmental procedures, such as keeping inventory records, filling out forms to initiate new purchases, checking purchase orders, and dealing with vendors. With more experience, they gain responsibility for selecting vendors and purchasing products. Agents may become *junior buyers* of standard catalog items, *assistant buyers,* or managers, perhaps with overall responsibility for purchasing, warehousing, traffic, and related functions. The top positions are *head of purchasing, purchasing director, materials manager, and vice-president of purchasing.* These positions include responsibilities concerning production, planning, and marketing.

Many agents advance by changing employers. Frequently an assistant purchasing agent for one firm will be hired as a purchasing agent or head of the purchasing department by another company.

Earnings

How much a buyer earns depends on various factors, including the employer's sales volume. Mass merchandisers, such as discount or chain department stores, pay among the highest salaries.

In 1998, earnings for buyers ranged from about $23,960 for the lowest 10 percent to more than $74,050 for the top 10 percent. Average salaries ranged from $29,660 to $49,660. In addition to their salaries, buyers often receive cash bonuses based on performance and may be offered incentive plans, such as profit sharing and stock options. Most buyers receive the usual company benefits, such as vacation, sick leave, life and health insurance, and pension plans. They generally also receive an employee's discount of 10 to 20 percent on merchandise purchased for personal use.

According to *Purchasing* magazine's 1998 salary survey, the average annual salary for purchasing agents was $54,700. The lowest paid purchasing professional made $15,000 while the highest paid earned $530,000. Nearly half of the survey respondents said they received bonuses as part of their compensation. The survey also found that bigger companies pay more, service buyers earn the most, and the chemical industry pays best. In addition, according to the survey, college graduates fill the highest ranking positions, have the greatest purchasing responsibilities, work for the largest companies, and generally earn the highest average annual compensation.

Work Environment

Working conditions for a purchasing agent are similar to those of other office employees. They usually work in rooms that are pleasant, well lighted, and clean. Work is year-round and generally steady because it is not particularly influenced by seasonal factors. Most have 40-hour workweeks, although overtime is not uncommon. In addition to regular hours, agents may have to attend meetings, read, prepare reports, visit suppliers' plants, or travel. While most work is done indoors, some agents occasionally need to inspect goods outdoors or in warehouses.

It is important for purchasing agents to have good working relations with others. They must interact closely with suppliers as well as with personnel in other departments of the company. Because of the importance of their decisions, purchasing agents sometimes work under great pressure.

Outlook

The number of purchasing agents is likely to grow more slowly than the average rate for all occupations through 2008. Computerized purchasing methods and the increased reliance on a select number of suppliers boost the productivity of purchasing personnel and reduce the number of new job openings. But as more and more hospitals, schools, state and local governments, and other service-related organizations turn to professional purchasing agents to help reduce costs, they will become good sources of employment. Nevertheless, most job openings will be to replace workers who retire or otherwise leave their jobs.

Demand will be strongest for those with a master's degree in business administration or an undergraduate degree in purchasing. Among firms manufacturing complex machinery, chemicals, and other technical products, the demand will be for graduates with a master's degree in engineering, another field of science, or business administration. Graduates of two-year programs in purchasing or materials management should continue to find good opportunities, especially in smaller companies.

For More Information

For materials on educational programs in the retail industry, contact:

National Retail Federation
325 7th Street, NW, Suite 1100
Washington, DC 20004
Tel: 202-783-7971
Web: http://www.nrf.com

For career information, send request marked "Careers" to:

American Purchasing Society
30 West Downer Place
Aurora, IL 60506
Tel: 630-859-0250
Web: http://www.american-purchasing.com/index2.htm

For career information and lists of colleges with purchasing programs, contact:

National Association of Purchasing Management
PO Box 22160
Tempe, AZ 85285-2160
Tel: 800-888-6276
Web: http://www.napm.org

For an information packet on purchasing careers in government, contact:

National Institute of Government Purchasing, Inc.
151 Spring Street
Herndon, VA 20170-5223
Tel: 800-FOR-NIGP
Web: http://www.nigp.org

Retail Business Owners

	School Subjects
Business Mathematics	

	Personal Skills
Helping/teaching Technical/scientific	

	Work Environment
Primarily indoors Primarily one location	

	Minimum Education Level
High school diploma	

	Salary Range
$15,000 to $35,000 to $100,000+	

	Certification or Licensing
None available	

	Outlook
About as fast as the average	

Overview

Retail business owners are entrepreneurs who start or buy their own businesses or franchise operations. They are responsible for all aspects of a business operation, from planning and ordering merchandise to overseeing day-to-day operations. Retail business owners sell such items as clothing, household appliances, groceries, jewelry, and furniture.

History

Retailing is a vital commercial activity, providing customers with an opportunity to purchase goods and services from various types of merchants. The first retail outlets in America were trading posts and general stores. At trading posts, goods obtained from Native Americans were exchanged for items imported from Europe or manufactured in other parts of the country. As villages and towns grew, trading posts developed into general stores and began to sell food, farm necessities, and clothing. Typically run by a single person, these stores sometimes served as the post office and became the social and economic center of their communities.

Since World War II, giant supermarkets, discount houses, chain stores, and shopping malls have grown popular. Even so, individually owned businesses still thrive, often giving customers more personal and better informed service. Moreover, despite the large growth in retail outlets and the increased competition that has accompanied it, retailing still provides the same basic, important function it did in the early years of the United States.

The Job

Although retail business owners sell a wide variety of products, from apples to automobiles, the basic job responsibilities remain the same. Simply stated, the retail business owner must do everything necessary to ensure the successful operation of a business.

There are five major categories of job responsibilities within a retail establishment: merchandising and buying, store operations, sales promotion and advertising, bookkeeping and accounting, and personnel supervision. *Merchandising and buying* determine the type and amount of actual goods to be sold. *Store operations* involve maintaining the building and providing for the movement of goods and personnel within the building. *Sales promotion and advertising* are the marketing methods used to inform customers and potential customers about the goods and services that are available. In *bookkeeping and accounting*, records are kept of payroll, taxes, and money spent and received. *Personnel* involves staffing the store with people who are trained and qualified to handle all the work that needs to be done.

The owner must be aware of all aspects of the business operation so that informed decisions can be made. Specific duties of an individual owner depend on the size of the store and the number of employees. In a store with more than 10 employees, many of the operational, promotional, and personnel activities may be supervised by a manager. The owner may plan the overall purpose and function of the store and hire a manager to oversee the day-to-day operations. In a smaller store, the owner may also do much of the operational activities, including sweeping the floor, greeting customers, and balancing the accounting books.

In both large and small operations, an owner must keep up to date on product information, as well as on economic and technological conditions that may have an impact on business. This entails reading catalogs about product availability, checking current inventories and prices, and researching and implementing any technological advances that may make the operation more efficient. For example, an owner may decide to purchase data processing equipment to help with accounting functions, as well as to generate a mailing list to inform customers of special sales.

Because of the risks involved in opening a business and the many economic and managerial demands put on individual owners, a desire to open a retail business should be combined with proper management skills, sufficient economic backing, and a good sense of what the public wants. The large majority of retail businesses fail because of a lack of managerial experience on the part of owners.

Franchise ownership, whereby an individual owner obtains a license to sell an existing company's goods or services, grew phenomenally during the 1980s. Franchise agreements enable the person who wants to open a business to have expert advice from the sponsoring company about location, hiring and training of employees, arrangement of merchandise, display of goods, and record keeping. Some entrepreneurs, however, do not want to be limited to the product lines and other restrictions that accompany running a franchise store. Franchise operations also may fail, but their likelihood of success is greater than that of a totally independent retail store.

Requirements

High School

A high school diploma is important in order to understand the basics of business ownership, though there are no specific educational or experiential requirements for this position. Course work in business administration is helpful, though, as is previous experience in the retail trade. Hard work, constant analysis and evaluation, and sufficient capital are important elements of a successful business venture.

High school students interested in owning a business should take courses in mathematics, business management, and any of a variety of business-related subjects, such as accounting, typing, and computer science. In addition, English and other courses enhancing communications skills should be pursued. Specific skill areas also should be developed. A person who wants to open an electronics repair shop, for example, should study as much about electronics as possible.

Owners of small retail businesses often manage the store and work behind the counter. In such case, the owner of a meat market is the butcher as well.

Postsecondary Training

As the business environment gets more and more competitive, many people are opting for an academic degree as a way of getting more training. An undergraduate college program emphasizing business communications, marketing, business law, business management, and accounting should be pursued. Some people choose to get a master's in business administration (MBA) or other related graduate degree. There are also special business schools that offer a one- or two-year program in business management. Some correspondence schools also offer courses on how to plan and run a business.

Other Requirements

Whatever the experience and training, a retail business owner needs a lot of energy, patience, and fortitude to overcome the slow times and other difficulties involved in running a business. Other important personal characteristics include maturity, creativity, and good business judgment. Retail business owners also should be able to motivate employees and delegate authority.

Although there are no special licenses or certificates needed to open a business, individual states or communities may have zoning codes or other regulations specifying what type of business can be located in a particular area. Owners should contact the appropriate city or municipality to determine any relevant regulations.

Exploring

Working full or part time as a sales clerk or in some other capacity within a retail business is a good way to learn about the responsibilities of operating a business. Talking with owners of small shops also is helpful, as is reading periodicals that publish articles on self-employment, such as *Entrepreneur* magazine (http://www.entrepreneurmag.com).

Most communities have a chamber of commerce whose members usually will be glad to share their insights into the career of a retail business owner. The Small Business Administration, an agency of the U.S. government, is another possible source of information.

Starting Out

Few people start their career as an owner. Many start as a manager or in some other position within a retail business. While developing managerial skills or while pursuing a college degree or other relevant training, you should decide what type of business you would like to own. Many people decide to buy an existing business because it already has a proven track record and because banks and other lending institutions often are more likely to loan money to an existing facility. A retail business owner should anticipate having at least 50 percent of the money needed to start or buy a business. Some people find it helpful to have one or more partners in a business venture.

Owning a franchise is another way of starting a business without a large capital investment, as franchise agreements often involve some assistance in planning and start-up costs. Franchise operations, however, are not necessarily less expensive to run than a totally independent business.

Advancement

Because an owner is by definition the boss, there are limited opportunities for advancement. Advancement often takes the form of expansion of an existing business, leading to increased earnings and prestige. Expanding a business also can entail added risk, as it involves increasing operational costs. A successful franchise owner may be offered an additional franchise location or an executive position at the corporate headquarters.

A small number of successful independent business owners choose to franchise their business operations in different areas. Some owners become part-time consultants, while others teach a course at a college or university or in an adult education program. This teaching often is done not only for the financial rewards but as a way of helping others investigate the option of retail ownership.

Earnings

Earnings vary widely and are greatly influenced by the ability of the individual owner, the type of product or service being sold, and existing economic conditions Some retail business owners may earn only about $15,000 a year, while the most successful earn $100,000 or more.

Work Environment

Retail business owners generally work in pleasant surroundings. Even so, ownership is a demanding occupation, with owners often working six or seven days a week. Working more than 60 hours a week is not unusual, especially during the Christmas season and other busy times. An owner of a large establishment may be able to leave a manager in charge of many parts of the business, but the owner still must be available to solve any pressing concerns. Owners of small businesses often stay in the store throughout the day, spending much of the time on their feet.

A retail business owner may occasionally travel out of town to attend conferences or to solicit new customers and product information. An owner of a small business, especially, should develop a close relationship with steady customers.

Outlook

There are more than 175,000 retail business owners in the United States. Employment is expected to grow about as fast as the average for all occupations through 2008.

The retail field is extremely competitive, and many businesses fail each year. The most common reason for failure is poor management. Thus people with some managerial experience or training will likely have the best chance at running a successful business.

For More Information

For a business starter packet with information about their loan program and ser-vices, and basic facts about starting a business, contact:

U.S. Small Business Administration
409 Third Street, SW
Washington, DC 20416
Tel: 800-827-5722
Web: http://www.sbaonline.sba.gov/

The following foundation conducts research and analysis of women-owned businesses.

National Foundation for Women Business Owners
1411 K Street, NW, Suite 1350
Washington, DC 20005-3407
Tel: 202-638-3060
Email: NFWBO@worldnet.att.net
Web: http://www.nfwbo.org/

For materials on educational programs in the retail industry, contact:

National Retail Federation
325 7th Street, NW, Suite 1000
Washington, DC 20004
Tel: 202-783-7971
Web: http://www.nrf.com

Retail Managers

School Subjects
Business
Mathematics

Personal Skills
Helping/teaching
Leadership/management

Work Environment
Primarily indoors
Primarily one location

Minimum Education Level
High school diploma

Salary Range
$16,700 to $40,000 to $100,000+

Certification or Licensing
None available

Outlook
More slowly than the average

Overview

Retail managers are responsible for the profitable operation of retail trade establishments. They oversee the selling of food, clothing, furniture, sporting goods, novelties, and many other items. Their duties include hiring, training, and supervising other employees, maintaining the physical facilities, managing inventory, monitoring expenditures and receipts, and maintaining good public relations.

History

In the United States, small, family-owned stores have been around for centuries. The first large chain store began to operate in the late 19th century. One of the aims of early chain stores was to provide staples for the pioneers of the newly settled West. Because chain store corporations were able to buy goods in large quantities and store them in warehouses, they were able to undersell private merchants.

The number of retail stores, especially supermarkets, began to grow rapidly during the 1930s. Stores often were owned and operated by chain corporations, which were able to benefit from bulk buying and more sophisticated storage practices. Cheaper transportation also contributed to the growth of retail stores because goods could be shipped and sold more economically.

Unlike the early family-owned stores, giant retail outlets employed large numbers of people, requiring various levels of management to oversee the business. Retail managers were hired to oversee particular areas within department stores, for example, but higher-level managers also were needed to make more general decisions about a company's goals and policies. Today, retailing is one of the nation's largest industries, employing more than five million people.

The Job

Retail managers are responsible for every phase of a store's operation. They often are one of the first employees to arrive in the morning and the last to leave at night. Their duties include hiring, training, and supervising other employees, maintaining the physical facilities, managing inventory, monitoring expenditures and receipts, and maintaining good public relations.

Perhaps the most important responsibility is hiring and training qualified employees. Managers then assign duties to employees, monitor their progress, promote employees, and increase salaries when appropriate. When an employee is not performing satisfactorily, a manager must find a way to improve the performance or, if necessary, fire him or her.

Managers should be good at working with people. Differences of opinion and personality clashes among employees are inevitable, and the manager must be able to restore good feelings among the staff. Managers often have to deal with customers' grievances and must attempt to restore goodwill toward the store when customers are dissatisfied.

Retail managers keep accurate and up-to-date records of store inventory. When new merchandise arrives, the manager ensures items are recorded, priced, and displayed or shelved. They must know when stock is getting low and order new items in a timely manner.

Some managers are responsible for advertising and merchandise promotions. The manager may confer with an advertising agency representative to determine appropriate advertising for the store. The manager also may decide what products to put on sale for advertising purposes.

The duties of store managers vary according to the type of merchandise sold, size of store, and number of employees. In small, owner-operated stores, managers often are involved in accounting, data processing, marketing, research, sales, and shipping. In large retail corporations, however, managers may be involved in only one or two activities.

Requirements

High School

A minimum high school education generally is required for this position. Helpful courses include English, mathematics, marketing, and economics.

Postsecondary Training

Most retail stores prefer applicants with a college degree, and many hire only college graduates. Liberal arts, social sciences, and business are the most common degrees held by retail managers.

To prepare for a career as a retail store manager, students should take courses in accounting, business, marketing, English, advertising, and computer science. If you are unable to attend college as a full-time student, you should consider obtaining a job in a store to gain experience and attend college part time. All managers, regardless of their education, must have good marketing, analytical, communications, and people skills.

Many large retail stores and national chains have established formal training programs, including classroom instruction, for their new employees. The training period may last a week or as long as one year. Training for a department store manager, for example, may include working as a salesperson in several departments in order to learn about the store's operations.

Other Requirements

A retail manager may put in very long hours. He or she should have good communication skills and enjoy working with and supervising people. Diplomacy often is necessary when creating schedules for workers and in disciplinary matters. There is a great deal of responsibility in retail management and such positions often are stressful. A calm disposition and ability to handle stress will serve the manager well.

Exploring

People interested in becoming retail managers may be able to find part-time, weekend, or summer jobs in a clothing store, supermarket, or other retail trade establishment. Students can gain valuable work experience through such jobs and will have the opportunity to observe the retail industry to determine whether they are interested in pursuing a career in it. It also is useful to read periodicals that publish articles on the retail field, such as *Stores* (http://www.stores.org), published by the National Retail Federation.

Employers

Nearly every type of retail business requires management, though small businesses may be run by their owners. Wherever retail sales are made there is an opportunity for a management position, though you may have to begin in a much lower job. The food industry employs more workers than nearly any other and retail food businesses always need managers, though smaller ones may not pay very well. In general, the larger the business and the bigger the city, the more you can earn.

Starting Out

Many new college graduates are able to find managerial positions through their schools' placement service. Some of the large retail chains engage in campus recruitment.

Not all store managers, however, are college graduates. Many store managers are promoted to their positions from jobs of less responsibility within the organization. Some may be in the retail industry for more than a dozen years before being promoted. Those with more education often receive promotions faster.

Regardless of educational background, people who are interested in the retail industry should consider working in a retail store at least part time or during the summer. Although there may not be an opening when the application is made, there often is a high turnover of employees in retail management, and vacancies occur from time to time.

Advancement

Advancement opportunities in retailing vary according to the size of the store, where the store is located, and the type of merchandise sold. Advancement also depends on the individual's work experience and educational background.

A store manager who works for a large retail chain, for example, may be given responsibility for a number of stores in a given area or region or transferred to a larger store in another city. Willingness to relocate to a new city may increase an employee's promotional opportunities.

Some managers decide to open their own stores after they have acquired enough experience in the retail industry. After working as a retail manager for a large chain of clothing stores, for example, a person may decide to open a small boutique.

Sometimes becoming a retail manager involves a series of promotions. A person who works in a supermarket, for example, may advance from clerk, checker, or bagger, to a regular assignment in one of several departments in the store. After a period of time, he or she may become an assistant manager and eventually, a manager.

Earnings

Salaries depend on the size of the store, the responsibilities of the job, and the number of customers served. Some managers earn as little as $16,700 but median earnings are about $29,570 in 1998, according to the *Occupational Outlook Handbook*. Experienced managers average about $40,000 and the top 10 percent earned more than $71,910 in 1998. Salaries in smaller stores are lower. Those who oversee an entire region for a retail chain can earn more than $100,000.

In addition to a salary, some stores offer their managers special bonuses, or commissions, which are typically connected to the store's performance. Many stores also offer employee discounts on store merchandise.

Work Environment

Most retail stores are pleasant places to work, and managers often are given comfortable offices. Many, however, work long hours. Managers often work six days a week and as many as 60 hours a week, especially during busy times of the year such as the Christmas season. Because holiday seasons are peak shopping periods, it is extremely rare that managers can take holidays off or schedule vacations around a holiday, even if the store is not open on that day.

Although managers usually can get away from the store during slack times, often they must be present if the store is open at night. It is important that the manager be available to handle the store's daily receipts, which usually are put in a safe or taken to a bank's night depository at the close of the business day.

Outlook

Employment of retail managers is expected to grow more slowly than the average for all occupations through 2008. Although retailers have reduced their management staff to cut costs and make operations more efficient, there still are good opportunities in retailing. However, competition for jobs probably will continue to increase, and computerized systems for inventory control may reduce the need for some managers. Applicants with the best educational backgrounds and work experience will have the best chances of finding jobs.

For More Information

For materials on educational programs in the retail industry, contact:

National Retail Federation
325 7th Street, NW, Suite 1000
Washington, DC 20004
Tel: 202-783-7971
Web: http://www.nrf.com

For a copy of How Many People Does It Take to Sell a Lightbulb?, *which describes jobs in retail, contact:*

International Mass Retail Association
1700 North Moore Street, Suite 2250
Arlington, VA 22209
Tel: 703-841-1184
Web: http://www.imra.org

Retail Sales Workers

School Subjects
English
Mathematics
Speech

Personal Skills
Helping/teaching
Communication/ideas

Work Environment
Primarily indoors
Primarily one location

Minimum Education Level
High school diploma

Salary Range
$8,840 to $18,096 to $31,800

Certification or Licensing
None available

Outlook
About as fast as the average

Overview

Retail sales workers assist customers with purchases by identifying their needs, showing or demonstrating merchandise, receiving payment, recording sales, and wrapping their purchases or arranging for their delivery. They are sometimes called *sales clerks, retail clerks,* or *salespeople.*

History

The development of retailing has paralleled the growth of civilization. When planning their cities, the Greeks and Romans established large marketplaces where individual merchants could display and sell their wares. As Europe emerged from the Middle Ages, organized trade began again with the development of medieval fairs. During the 13th century, more than three thousand fairs were held on a regular basis. By the 15th century, weekly markets in various cities began to replace the fairs.

As specialization in manufacture developed, the medieval artisan appeared. The artisans were craft workers, such as weavers and metalsmiths, who sold the products they made. Most of the goods they produced were made after they received a specific order from a customer.

The Industrial Revolution and its techniques of mass production encouraged the development of specialized retail establishments. The first retail outlets in the United States were trading posts and general stores. At trading posts, goods obtained from Native Americans were exchanged for items imported from Europe or manufactured in the eastern United States. Trading posts had to be located on the fringes of settlements and relocated to follow the westward movement of the frontier. As villages and towns grew, what had been trading posts frequently developed into general stores. General stores sold food staples, farm necessities, and clothing. They often served as the local post office and became the social and economic centers of their communities. They were sometimes known as dry goods stores.

A number of changes occurred in the retail field during the second half of the 19th century. The growth of specialized retail stores (such as hardware, feed, grocery, and drug stores) reflected the growing sophistication of available products and customer tastes. The first grocery chain store, which started in New York City in 1859, led to a new concept in retailing. Later, merchants such as Marshall Field developed huge department stores, so named because of their large number of separate departments. Their variety of merchandise, ability to advertise their products, and low selling prices contributed to the rapid growth and success of these stores. Retail sales workers staffed the departments, and for the public they became the stores' primary representatives.

The 20th century witnessed the birth of supermarkets and suburban shopping centers, the emergence of discount houses, and the expansion of credit buying. Today, retailing is the second largest industry in the United States. Grocery stores and chains have the highest annual sales in the retail field—followed, in order of size, by automobile dealers, department stores, restaurants and cafeterias, lumber and building suppliers, drug and proprietary stores, furniture stores, variety stores, liquor stores, hardware stores, and jewelry stores. All of these retailers hire sales workers.

The Job

Salespeople work in more than a hundred different types of retail establishments in a variety of roles. Some, for example, work in small specialty shops where, in addition to waiting on customers, they might check inventory, order stock from sales representatives (or by telephone or mail), place newspaper display advertisements, prepare window displays, and rearrange merchandise for sale.

Other salespeople may work in specific departments, such as the furniture department, of a large department store. The employees in a department work in shifts to provide service to customers six or seven days a week. To improve their sales effectiveness and knowledge of merchandise, they attend regular staff meetings. The work of retail salespeople is supported by advertising, window decorating, sales promotion, buying, and market research specialists.

Whatever they are selling, the primary responsibility of retail sales workers is to interest customers in the merchandise. This might be done by describing the product's features, demonstrating its use, or showing various models and colors. Some retail sales workers must have specialized knowledge, particularly those who sell such expensive, complicated products as stereos, appliances, and personal computers.

In addition to selling, most retail sales workers make out sales checks; receive cash, check, and charge payments; bag or package purchases; and give change and receipts. Depending on the hours they work, retail sales workers might have to open or close the cash register. This might include counting the money in the cash register; separating charge slips, coupons, and exchange vouchers; and making deposits at the cash office. The sales records they keep are normally used in inventory control. Sales workers are often held responsible for the contents of their registers, and repeated shortages are cause for dismissal in many organizations.

Sales workers must be aware of any promotions the store is sponsoring and know the store's policies and procedures, especially on returns and exchanges. Also, they often must recognize possible security risks and know how to handle such situations.

Consumers often form their impressions of a store by its sales force. To stay ahead in the fiercely competitive retail industry, employers are increasingly stressing the importance of providing courteous and efficient service. When a customer wants an item that is not on the sales floor, for example, the sales worker might be expected to check the stockroom and, if necessary, place a special order or call another store to locate the item.

Requirements

High School

Employers generally prefer to hire high school graduates for most sales positions. Such subjects as English, speech, and mathematics provide a good background for these jobs. Many high schools and two-year colleges have special programs that include courses in merchandising, principles of retailing, and retail selling.

Postsecondary Training

In retail sales, as in other fields, the level of opportunity tends to coincide with the level of a person's education. In many stores, college graduates enter immediately into on-the-job training programs to prepare them for management assignments. Successful and experienced workers who do not have a degree might also qualify for these programs. Useful college courses include economics, business administration, and marketing. Many colleges offer majors in retailing. Executives in many companies express a strong preference for liberal arts graduates, especially those with some business courses or a master's degree in business administration.

Other Requirements

The retail sales worker must be in good health. Many selling positions require standing most of the day. The sales worker must have stamina to face the grueling pace of busy times, such as weekends and the Christmas season, while at the same time remaining pleasant and effective. Personal appearance is important. Salespeople should be neat and well groomed and have an outgoing personality.

A pleasant speaking voice, natural friendliness, tact, and patience are all helpful personal characteristics. The sales worker must be able to converse easily with strangers of all ages. In addition to interpersonal skills, sales workers must be equally good with figures. They should be able to add and subtract accurately and quickly and operate cash registers and other types of business machines.

Most states have established minimum standards that govern retail employment. Some states set a minimum age of 14, require at least a high school diploma, or prohibit more than eight hours of work a day or 48 hours in any six days. These requirements are often relaxed for those people employed during the Christmas season.

Exploring

Because of its seasonal nature, retailing offers numerous opportunities for temporary or part-time sales experience. Most stores add extra personnel for the Christmas season. Vacation areas may hire sales employees, usually high school or college students. Fewer sales positions are available in metropolitan areas during the summer, as this is frequently the slowest time of the year.

Many high schools and junior colleges have developed "distributive education" programs that combine courses in retailing with part-time work in the field. The distributive education student may receive academic credit for this work experience in addition to regular wages. Store owners cooperating in these programs often hire students as full-time personnel upon completion of the program.

Employers

There are more than a hundred different types of retail establishments. Among these are small specialty shops, large department stores, retail chains, and drug, variety, and grocery stores. Sales workers are needed in all of these.

Starting Out

If they have openings, retail stores usually hire beginning salespeople who come in and fill out an application. Major department stores maintain extensive personnel departments, while in smaller stores the manager might do the hiring. Occasionally, sales applicants are given an aptitude test.

Young people might be hired immediately for sales positions. Often, however, they begin by working in the stockroom as clerks, helping to set up merchandise displays, or assisting in the receiving or shipping departments. After a while they might be moved up to a sales assignment.

Training varies with the type and size of the store. In large stores, the beginner might benefit from formal training courses that discuss sales techniques, store policies, the mechanics of recording sales, and an overview of the entire store. Programs of this type are usually followed by on-the-job sales supervision. The beginner in a small store might receive personal instruction from the manager or a senior sales worker, followed by supervised sales experience.

College graduates and people with successful sales experience often enter executive training programs (sometimes referred to as "flying squads" because they move rapidly through different parts of the store). As they rotate through various departments, the trainees are exposed to merchandising methods, stock and inventory control, advertising, buying, credit, and personnel. By spending time in each of these areas, trainees receive a broad retailing background designed to help them as they advance into the ranks of management.

Advancement

Large stores have the most opportunities for promotion. Retailing, however, is a mobile field, and successful and experienced people can readily change employment. This is one of the few fields where, if the salesperson has the necessary initiative and ability, advancement to executive positions is possible regardless of education.

When first on the job, sales workers develop their career potential by specializing in a particular line of merchandise. They become authorities on a certain product line, such as sporting equipment, women's suits, or building materials. Many good sales workers prefer the role of the senior sales worker and remain at this level. Others might be asked to become supervisor of a section. Eventually they might develop into a department manager, floor manager, division or branch manager, or general manager.

People with sales experience often enter related areas, such as buying. Other retail store workers advance into support areas, such as personnel, accounting, public relations, and credit.

Young people with ability find that retailing offers the opportunity for unusually rapid advancement. One study revealed that half of all retail executives are under 35 years of age. It is not uncommon for a person under 35 to be in charge of a retail store or department with an annual sales volume of over $1,000,000. Conversely, the retail executive who makes bad merchandising judgments might quickly be out of a job.

Earnings

Most beginning sales workers start at the federal minimum wage, which is currently $5.15 an hour. Wages vary greatly, depending primarily on the type of store and the degree of skill required. Businesses might offer higher wages to attract and retain workers. Some sales workers make as much as $12 an hour or more.

Department stores or retail chains might pay more than smaller stores. Higher wages are paid for positions requiring a greater degree of skill. Many sales workers also receive a commission (often 4 to 8 percent) on their sales or are paid solely on commission. According to the *Occupational Outlook Handbook*, sales workers earned the following average hourly earnings in 1997: women's clothing stores, $6.20; department stores, $6.90, and new and used car dealers, $15.10.

Salespeople in many retail stores are allowed a discount on their own purchases, ranging from 10 to 25 percent. This privilege is sometimes extended to the worker's family. Meals in the employee cafeterias maintained by large stores might be served at a price that is below cost. Many stores provide sick leave, medical and life insurance, and retirement benefits. Most stores give paid vacations.

Work Environment

Retail sales workers generally work in clean, comfortable, well-lighted areas. Those with seniority have reasonably good job security. When business is slow, stores might curtail hiring and not fill vacancies that occur. Most stores, however, are able to weather mild business recessions without having to release experienced sales workers. During periods of economic recession, competition among salespeople for job openings can become intense.

With nearly two million retail stores across the country, sales positions are found in every region. An experienced salesperson can find employment in almost any state. The vast majority of positions, however, are located in large cities or suburban areas.

The 5-day, 40-hour workweek is the exception rather than the rule in retailing. Most salespeople can expect to work some evening and weekend hours, and longer than normal hours might be scheduled during Christmas and other peak periods. In addition, most retailers restrict the use of vacation time between Thanksgiving and early January. Most sales workers receive overtime pay during Christmas and other rush seasons. Part-time salespeople generally work at peak hours of business, supplementing the full-time staff. Because competition in the retailing business is keen, many retailers work under pressure. The sales worker might not be directly involved but will feel the pressures of the industry in subtle ways. The sales worker must be able to adjust to alternating periods of high activity and dull monotony. No two days—or even customers—are alike. Because some customers are hostile and rude, salespeople must learn to exercise tact and patience at all times.

Outlook

In 1998, about 4.6 million people were employed as sales workers in retail stores of all types and sizes. The employment of sales personnel should grow about as fast as the average for all occupations through 2008. Turnover among sales workers is much higher than average. Many of the expected employment opportunities will stem from the need to replace workers. Other positions will result from existing stores' staffing for longer business hours or reducing the length of the average employee workweek.

Several factors—the full effects of which have yet to be measured—might reduce the long-range demand for sales personnel. As drug, variety, grocery, and other stores rapidly convert to self-service operations, they will need fewer sales workers. In contrast, many other stores are trying to stay competitive by offering better customer service and more sales staff attention.

At the same time, many products (such as stereo components, electrical appliances, computers, and sporting goods) do not lend themselves to self-service operations. These products require extremely skilled sales workers to assist customers and explain the benefits of various makes and models. On balance, as easy-to-sell goods will be increasingly marketed in self-service stores, the demand in the future will be strongest for sales workers who are knowledgeable about particular types of products.

During economic recessions, sales volume and the resulting demand for sales workers generally decline. Purchases of costly items, such as cars, appliances, and furniture, tend to be postponed during difficult economic times. In areas of high unemployment, sales of all types of goods might decline. Since turnover of sales workers is usually very high, however, employers often can cut payrolls simply by not replacing all those who leave.

There should continue to be good opportunities for temporary and part-time workers, especially during the holidays. Stores are particularly interested in people who, by returning year after year, develop good sales backgrounds.

For More Information

For materials on educational programs in the retail industry, contact:

National Retail Federation
325 7th Street, NW, Suite 1000
Washington, DC 20004
Tel: 202-783-7971
Web: http://www.nrf.com

Sales Representatives

School Subjects	Business Mathematics
Personal Skills	Communication/ideas Helping/teaching
Work Environment	Indoors and outdoors Primarily multiple locations
Minimum Education Level	High school diploma
Salary Range	$19,220 to $36,540 to $100,000+
Certification or Licensing	None available
Outlook	Little change or more slowly than the average

Overview

Sales representatives, also called *sales reps,* sell the products and services of manufacturers and wholesalers. They look for potential customers or clients such as retail stores, other manufacturers or wholesalers, government agencies, hospitals, and other institutions; explain or demonstrate their products to these clients; and attempt to make a sale. The job may include follow-up calls and visits to ensure the customer is satisfied.

Sales representatives work under a variety of titles. Those employed by manufacturers are typically called *manufacturers' sales workers* or *manufacturers' representatives.* Those who work for wholesalers are sometimes called *wholesale trade sales workers* or *wholesale sales representatives.* A *manufacturers' agent* is a self-employed salesperson who agrees to represent the products of various companies. A *door-to-door sales worker* usually represents just one company and sells products directly to consumers, typically in their homes.

History

Sales representatives for manufacturers and wholesalers have long played an important role in the U.S. economy. By representing products and seeking out potential customers, they have helped in the efficient distribution of large amounts of merchandise.

The earliest wholesalers were probably the ship "chandlers," or suppliers, of colonial New England, who assembled in large quantities the food and equipment required by merchant ships and military vessels. Ship owners found that a centralized supply source enabled them to equip their vessels quickly.

Various changes in the 19th century made wholesalers more prominent. Factories were becoming larger, thus allowing for huge amounts of merchandise to be manufactured or assembled in a single location. New forms of transportation, especially the railroad, made it more practical for manufacturers to sell their products over great distances. Although some manufacturers would sell their goods directly to retail outlets and elsewhere, many found it easier and more profitable to let wholesalers do this job. Retail stores, moreover, liked working with wholesalers, who were able to sell them a wide range of merchandise from different manufacturers and from different areas of the country and the world.

The sales representatives hired by manufacturers and wholesalers were typically given a specific territory in which to sell their goods. Armed with illustrated product catalogs, special promotional deals, and financial support for advertising, they traveled to prospective customers and tried to explain the important qualities of their products. Competition between sales representatives sometimes was fierce, leading some to be less than scrupulous. Product claims were exaggerated, and retail stores were sometimes supplied with shoddy merchandise. Eventually more fact-based sales pitches were emphasized by manufacturers and wholesalers, who in the long run benefited from having responsible, honest, well-informed representatives. Products also began to be backed by written guarantees of quality.

Meanwhile, some manufacturers were employing door-to-door sales workers to sell their products directly to consumers. Direct selling in the United States goes back to the famous "Yankee Peddler" who, during colonial times, traveled by wagon, on horseback, and sometimes on foot, bringing to isolated settlers many products that were not easily available otherwise. A forerunner of the modern door-to-door sales worker, peddlers also tried to anticipate the settlers' needs and wants. They frequently represented new or unknown products with the hope of creating a demand for them.

Changes in the 20th century, once again including improvements in transportation, brought still more possibilities for sales representatives. Automobiles allowed representatives to travel to many more communities and to carry more product samples and descriptive catalogs. Trucks provided a new means of transporting merchandise. The growth of commercial aviation further expanded the opportunities for salespeople. Sales representatives would eventually be able to travel to customers in New York, Atlanta, Los Angeles, and Minneapolis, for example, all during a single week.

By the late 20th century, the food products industry was one of the largest employers of sales representatives. Other important fields included printing, publishing, fabricated metal products, chemicals and dyes, electrical and other machinery, and transportation equipment. Among the many establishments helped by sales representatives were retail outlets, who needed a constant supply of clothing, housewares, and other consumer goods, and hospitals, who purchased specialized surgical instruments, drugs, rubber gloves, and thousands of other products from representatives.

The Job

Manufacturers' representatives and wholesale sales representatives sell goods to retail stores, other manufacturers and wholesalers, government agencies, and various institutions. They usually do so within a specific geographical area. Some representatives concentrate on just a few products. An electrical appliance salesperson, for example, may sell 10 to 30 items ranging from food freezers and air-conditioners to waffle irons and portable heaters. Representatives of drug wholesalers, however, may sell as many as 50,000 items.

The duties of sales representatives usually include locating and contacting potential new clients, keeping a regular correspondence with existing customers, determining their clients' needs, and informing them of pertinent products and prices. They also travel to meet with clients, show them samples or catalogs, take orders, arrange for delivery, and possibly provide installation. A sales representative also must handle customer complaints, keep up to date on new products, and prepare reports. Many salespeople attend trade conferences, where they learn about products and make sales contacts.

Finding new customers is one of the most important tasks. Sales representatives often follow leads suggested by other clients, from advertisements in trade journals, and from participants in trade shows and conferences. They may make "cold calls" to potential clients. Sales representatives frequently meet with and entertain prospective clients during evenings and weekends.

Representatives who sell highly technical machinery or complex office equipment often are referred to as *sales engineers* or *industrial sales workers*. Because their products tend to be more specialized and their clients' needs more complex, the sales process for these workers tends to be longer and more involved. Before recommending a product, they may, for example, carefully analyze a customer's production processes, distribution methods, or office procedures. They usually prepare extensive sales presentations that include information on how their products will improve the quality and efficiency of the customer's operations.

Some sales engineers, often with the help of their company's research and development department, adapt products to a customer's specialized needs. They may provide the customer with instructions on how to use the new equipment or work with installation experts who provide this service. Some companies maintain a sales assistance staff to train customers and provide specific information. This permits sales representatives to devote a greater percentage of their time to direct sales contact.

Other sales workers, called *detail people*, do not engage in direct selling activities but strive instead to create a better general market for their companies' products. A detail person for a drug company, for example, may call on physicians and hospitals to inform them of new products and distribute samples.

The particular products sold by the sales representative directly affect the nature of the work. Salespeople who represent sporting goods manufacturers may spend most of their time driving from town to town calling on retail stores that carry sporting equipment. They may visit with coaches and athletic directors of high schools and colleges. A representative in this line may be a former athlete or coach who knows intimately the concerns of his or her customers.

Food manufacturers and wholesalers employ large numbers of sales representatives. Because these salespeople usually know the grocery stores and major chains that carry their products, their main focus is to ensure the maximum sales volume. Representatives negotiate with retail merchants to obtain the most advantageous store and shelf position for displaying their products. They encourage the store or chain to advertise their products, sometimes by offering to pay part of the advertising costs or by reducing the selling price to the merchant so that a special sale price can be offered to customers. Representatives check to make sure that shelf items are neatly arranged and that the store has sufficient stock of their products.

Sales transactions can involve huge amounts of merchandise, sometimes worth millions of dollars. For example, in a single transaction, a washing-machine manufacturer, construction company, or automobile manufacturer may purchase all the steel products it needs for an extended period of time.

Salespeople in this field may do much of their business by telephone because the product they sell is standardized and, to the usual customer, requires no particular description or demonstration.

Direct, or door-to-door, selling has been an effective way of marketing various products, such as appliances and housewares, cookware, china, tableware and linens, foods, drugs, cosmetics and toiletries, costume jewelry, clothing, and greeting cards. Like other sales representatives, door-to-door sales workers find prospective buyers, explain and demonstrate their products, and take orders. Door-to-door selling has waned in popularity, and Internet selling has taken over much of the door-to-door market.

Several different arrangements are common between companies and their door-to-door sales workers. Under the "direct company plan," for example, a sales representative is authorized to take orders for a product, and the company pays the representative a commission for each completed order. Such workers may be employees of the company and may receive a salary in addition to a commission, or they may be independent contractors. They usually are very well trained. Sales workers who sell magazine subscriptions may be hired, trained, and supervised by a *subscription crew leader*, who assigns representatives to specific areas, reviews the orders they take, and compiles sales records.

Under the "exhibit plan" a salesperson sets up an exhibit booth at a place where large numbers of people are expected to pass, such as a state fair, trade show, or product exposition. Customers approach the booth and schedule appointments with the salespersons for later demonstrations at home.

The "dealer plan" allows a salesperson to function as the proprietor of a small business. The salesperson, or dealer, purchases the product wholesale from the company and then resells it to consumers at the retail price, mainly through door-to-door sales.Under various "group plans," a customer is contacted by a salesperson and given the opportunity to sponsor a sales event. In the "party plan," for example, the sales representative arranges to demonstrate products at the home of a customer, who then invites a group of friends for the "party." The customer who hosts the party receives free or discounted merchandise in return for the use of the home and for assembling other potential customers for the salesperson.

Finally, the "COD plan" allows representatives to sell products on a cash-on-delivery (COD) basis. In this method, the salesperson makes a sale, perhaps collecting an advance deposit, and sends the order to the company. The company, in turn, ships the merchandise directly to the customer, who in this case makes payment to the delivery person, or to the salesperson, who then delivers the product to the customer and collects the balance owed.

Whatever the sales plan, door-to-door sales workers have some advantages over their counterparts in retail stores. Direct sellers, for example, do not have to wait for the customer to come to them; they go out and find the buyers for their products. The direct seller often carries only one product or a limited line of products and thus is much more familiar with the features and benefits of the merchandise. In general, direct sellers get the chance to demonstrate their products where they will most likely be used—in the home.

There are drawbacks to this type of selling. Many customers grow impatient or hostile when salespeople come to their house unannounced and uninvited. It may take several visits to persuade someone to buy the product. In a brief visit, the direct seller must win the confidence of the customer, develop the customer's interest in a product or service, and close the sale.

Requirements

High School

A high school diploma is required for most sales positions, although an increasing number of salespeople are graduates of two- or four-year colleges.

Postsecondary Training

The more complex a product, the greater the likelihood that it will be sold by a college-trained person. About 30 percent of all door-to-door sales workers have a college degree.

Some areas of sales work require specialized college work. Those in engineering sales, for example, usually have a college degree in a relevant engineering field. Other fields that demand specific college degrees include chemical sales (chemistry or chemical engineering), office systems (accounting or business administration), and pharmaceuticals and drugs (biology, chemistry, or pharmacy). Those in less technical sales positions usually benefit from course work in English, speech, psychology, marketing, public relations, economics, advertising, finance, accounting, and business law.

Other Requirements

Sales representatives should enjoy working with people. Other important personal traits include self-confidence, enthusiasm, and self-discipline.

Exploring

A student interested in becoming a sales representative may benefit from part-time or summer work in a retail store. Working as a telemarketer also is useful. Some high schools and junior colleges offer programs that combine classroom study with work experience in sales.

Various opportunities exist that provide experience in direct selling. Students can take part in sales drives for school or community groups.

Occasionally manufacturers hire college students for summer assignments. These temporary positions provide an opportunity for the employer and employee to appraise each other. A high percentage of students hired for these specialized summer programs become career employees after graduation. Some wholesale warehouses also offer temporary or summer positions.

Employers

In the United States, 1.5 million people work as manufacturers' and wholesale sales representatives. About 75 percent work in wholesale, many as sellers of machinery. Food, drugs, electrical goods, hardware, and clothing are among the most common products sold by sales representatives.

Starting Out

Firms looking for sales representatives sometimes list openings with high school and college placement offices, as well as with public and private employment agencies. In many areas, professional sales associations refer people to suitable openings. Contacting companies directly also is recommended. A list of manufacturers and wholesalers can be found in telephone books and industry directories, which are available at public libraries.

Although some high school graduates are hired for manufacturers' or wholesale sales jobs, many join a company in a nonselling position, such as office, stock, or shipping clerk. This experience allows an employee to learn about the company and its products. From there, he or she eventually may be promoted to a sales position.

Most new representatives complete a training period before receiving a sales assignment. In some cases new salespeople rotate through several departments of an organization to gain a broad exposure to the company's products. Large companies often use formal training programs lasting two years or more, while small organizations frequently rely on supervised sales experience.

Direct selling usually is an easy field to enter. Direct sale companies advertise for available positions in newspapers, in sales workers' specialty magazines, and on television and radio. Many people enter direct selling through contacts they have had with other door-to-door sales workers. Most firms have district or area representatives who interview applicants and arrange the necessary training. Part-time positions in direct selling are common.

Advancement

New representatives usually spend their early years improving their sales ability, developing product knowledge, and finding new clients. As sales workers gain experience they may be shifted to increasingly large territories or more difficult types of customers. In some organizations, experienced sales workers narrow their focus. For example, an office equipment sales representative may work solely on government contracts.

Advancement to management positions, such as regional or district manager, also is possible. Some representatives, however, choose to remain in basic sales. Because of commissions, they often earn more money than their managers do, and many enjoy being in the field and working directly with their customers.

A small number of representatives decide to become manufacturers' agents, or self-employed salespeople who handle products for various organizations. Agents perform many of the same functions as sales representatives but usually on a more modest scale.

Door-to-door sales workers also have advancement possibilities. Some are promoted to supervisory roles and recruit, train, and manage new members of the sales force. Others become area, branch, or district managers. Many managers of direct selling firms began as door-to-door sales workers.

Earnings

Many beginning sales representatives are paid a salary while receiving their training. After assuming direct responsibility for a sales territory, they may receive only a commission (a fixed percentage of each dollar sold). Also common is a modified commission plan (a lower rate of commission on sales plus a low base salary). Some companies provide bonuses to successful representatives.

Because manufacturers' and wholesale sales representatives typically work on commission, salaries vary widely. Some made as little as $19,220 a year in 1998, according to the *Occupational Outlook Handbook*. More successful representatives earn more than $100,000. Most, however, earn between $26,350 and $51,580. The average salary is about $36,540.

Earnings can be affected by changes in the economy or industry cycles, and great fluctuations in salary from year to year or month to month are common. Employees who travel usually are reimbursed for transportation, hotels, meals, and client entertainment expenses.

Door-to-door sales workers usually earn a straight commission on their sales, ranging from 10 to 40 percent of an item's suggested retail price. A typical or average income for this occupation is hard to estimate. It is not uncommon, however, for an experienced, full-time door-to-door salesperson to make between $12,000 and $20,000 a year.

Sales representatives typically receive vacation days, medical and life insurance, and retirement benefits. However, manufacturers' agents and some door-to-door sales workers do not receive benefits.

Work Environment

Salespeople generally work long and irregular hours. Those with large territories may spend all day calling and meeting customers in one city and much of the night traveling to the place where they will make the next day's calls and visits. Sales workers with a small territory may do little overnight travel but, like most sales workers, may spend many evenings preparing reports, writing up orders, and entertaining customers. Several times a year, sales workers may travel to company meetings and participate in trade conventions and conferences. Irregular working hours, travel, and the competitive demands of the job can be disruptive to ordinary family life.

Sales work is physically demanding. Representatives often spend most of the day on their feet. Many carry heavy sample cases or catalogs. Occasionally, sales workers assist a customer in arranging a display of the company's products or moving stock items. Many door-to-door sellers work in their own community or nearby areas, although some cover more extensive and distant territories. They often are outdoors in all kinds of weather. Direct sellers must treat customers, even those who are rude or impatient, with tact and courtesy.

Outlook

Employment for manufacturers' and wholesale sales representatives is expected to grow more slowly than the average for all occupations through 2008. Technological advances have reduced the number of sales representatives needed to sell products. Electronic data interchange (EDI), a system that improves communication between computers, for example, allows customers to order goods from suppliers more easily.

Future opportunities will vary greatly depending upon the specific product and industry. For example, as giant food chains replace independent grocers, fewer salespeople will be needed to sell groceries to individual stores. By contrast, greater opportunities will probably exist in the air-conditioning field, and advances in consumer electronics and computer technology also may provide many new opportunities.

For More Information

For career information, including career brochures, a list of colleges that teach marketing, and a list of job titles, sources, and salaries, contact:

Direct Marketing Association
Direct Marketing Educational Foundation
1120 Avenue of the Americas
New York, NY 10036-6700
Tel: 212-768-7277
Web: http://www.the-dma.org/dmef/index.shtml

For referrals to industry trade associations, contact:

Manufacturers' Agents National Association
PO Box 3467
23016 Mill Creek Drive
Laguna Hills, CA 92654-3467
Tel: 949-859-4040
Email: MANA@MANAonline.org
Web: http://www.manaonline.org/

Stock Clerks

	School Subjects
English	
Mathematics	
	Personal Skills
Following instructions	
Helping/teaching	
	Work Environment
Primarily indoors	
Primarily one location	
	Minimum Education Level
High school diploma	
	Salary Range
$8,840 to $15,000 to $20,000	
	Certification or Licensing
None available	
	Outlook
Little change or more slowly than the average	

Overview

Stock clerks receive, unpack, store, distribute, and record the inventory for materials or products used by a company, plant, or store.

History

Almost every type of business establishment imaginable—shoe store, restaurant, hotel, auto repair shop, hospital, supermarket, or steel mill—buys materials or products from outside distributors and uses these materials in its operations. A large part of the company's money is tied up in these inventory stocks, but without them operations would come to a standstill. Stores would run out of merchandise to sell, mechanics would be unable to repair cars until new parts were shipped in, and factories would be unable to operate once their basic supply of raw materials ran out.

To avoid these problems, businesses have developed their own inventory-control systems to store enough goods and raw materials for uninterrupted operations, move these materials to the places they are needed, and know when it is time to order more. These systems are the responsibility of stock clerks.

The Job

Stock clerks work in just about every type of industry, and no matter what kind of storage or stock room they staff—food, clothing, merchandise, medicine, or raw materials—the work of stock clerks is essentially the same. They receive, sort, put away, distribute, and keep track of the items a business sells or uses. Their titles sometimes vary based on their responsibilities.

When goods are received in a stockroom, stock clerks unpack the shipment and check the contents against documents such as the invoice, purchase order, and bill of lading, which lists the contents of the shipment. The shipment is inspected, and any damaged goods are set aside. Stock clerks may reject or send back damaged items or call vendors to complain about the condition of the shipment. In large companies this work may be done by a shipping and receiving clerk.

Once the goods are received, stock clerks organize them and sometimes mark them with identifying codes or prices so they can be placed in stock according to the existing inventory system. In this way the materials or goods can be found readily when needed, and inventory control is much easier. In many firms stock clerks use hand-held scanners and computers to keep inventory records up to date.

In retail stores and supermarkets stock clerks may bring merchandise to the sales floor and stock shelves and racks. In stockrooms and warehouses they store materials in bins, on the floor, or on shelves. In other settings, such as restaurants, hotels, and factories, stock clerks deliver goods when they are needed. They may do this on a regular schedule or at the request of other employees or supervisors. Although many stock clerks use mechanical equipment, such as forklifts, to move heavy items, some perform strenuous and laborious work. In general, the work of a stock clerk involves much standing, bending, walking, stretching, lifting, and carrying.

When items are removed from the inventory, stock clerks adjust records to reflect the products' use. These records are kept as current as possible, and inventories are periodically checked against these records. Every item is counted, and the totals are compared with the records on hand or the records from the sales, shipping, production, or purchasing departments. This helps identify how fast items are being used, when items must be ordered from outside suppliers, or even whether items are disappearing from the stockroom. Many retail establishments use computerized cash registers that maintain an inventory count automatically as they record the sale of each item.

The duties of stock clerks vary depending on their place of employment. Stock clerks working in small firms perform many different tasks, including shipping and receiving, inventory control, and purchasing. In large firms, responsibilities may be more narrow. More specific job categories include inventory clerks, stock control clerks, material clerks, order fillers, merchandise distributors, and shipping and receiving clerks.

At a construction site or factory that uses a variety of raw and finished materials, there are many different types of specialized work for stock clerks. *Tool crib attendants* issue, receive, and store the various hand tools, machine tools, dies, and other equipment used in an industrial establishment. They make sure the tools come back in reasonably good shape and keep track of those that need replacing. *Parts order and stock clerks* purchase, store, and distribute the spare parts needed for motor vehicles and other industrial equipment. *Metal control coordinators* oversee the movement of metal stock and supplies used in producing nonferrous metal sheets, bars, tubing, and alloys. In mining and other industries that regularly use explosives, *magazine keepers* store explosive materials and components safely and distribute them to authorized personnel. In the military, *space and storage clerks* keep track of the weights and amounts of ammunition and explosive components stored in the magazines of an arsenal and check their storage condition.

Many types of stock clerks can be found in other industries. At printing companies, *cut-file clerks* collect, store, and hand out the layout cuts, ads, mats, and electrotypes used in the printing process. *Parts clerks* handle and distribute spare and replacement parts in repair and maintenance shops. In eyeglass centers, *prescription clerks* select the lens blanks and frames for making eyeglasses and keep inventory stocked at a specified level. In motion picture companies, *property custodians* receive, store, and distribute the props needed for shooting. In hotels and hospitals, *linen room attendants* issue and keep track of inventories of bed linen, table cloths, and uniforms, while *kitchen clerks* verify the quantity and quality of food products being taken from the storeroom to the kitchen. Aboard ships, the clerk in charge of receiving and issuing supplies and keeping track of inventory is known as the *storekeeper*.

Requirements

High School

Although there are no specific educational requirements for beginning stock clerks, employers prefer to hire high school graduates. Reading and writing skills and a basic knowledge of mathematics are necessary; typing and filing skills are also useful. In the future, as more companies install computerized inventory systems, a knowledge of computer operations will be important.

Other Requirements

Good health and good eyesight is important. A willingness to take orders from supervisors and others is necessary for this work, as is the ability to follow directions. Organizational skills also are important, as is neatness. Depending on where they work, some stock clerks may be required to join a union. This is especially true of stock clerks who are employed by industry and who work in large cities with a high percentage of union-affiliated companies.

When a stock clerk handles certain types of materials, extra training or certification may be required. Generally those who handle jewelry, liquor, or drugs must be bonded.

Exploring

The best way to learn about the responsibilities of a stock clerk is to get a part-time or summer job as a sales clerk, stockroom helper, stockroom clerk, or, in some factories, stock chaser. These jobs are relatively easy to get and can help students learn about stock work, as well as about the duties of workers in related positions. This sort of part-time work can also lead to a full-time job.

Employers

About 2.3 million people work as stock clerks. Of these, 60 percent work as stockroom, warehouse, or yard clerks, while 40 percent work as sales floor stock clerks. Many sales floor clerks work part-time. Almost 80 percent of stockroom, warehouse, and yard clerks work in retail and wholesale firms, and the remainder work in hospitals, factories, government agencies, schools, and other organizations. Nearly all sales floor stock clerks are employed in retail establishments, with about two-thirds working in supermarkets.

Starting Out

Job openings for stock clerks often are listed in newspaper classified ads. Job seekers should contact the personnel office of the firm looking for stock clerks and fill out an application for employment. School counselors, parents, relatives, and friends also can be good sources for job leads and may be able to give personal references if an employer requires them.

Stock clerks usually receive on-the-job training. New workers start with simple tasks, such as counting and marking stock. The basic responsibilities of the job are usually learned within the first few weeks. As they progress, stock clerks learn to keep records of incoming and outgoing materials, take inventories, and place orders. As wholesale and warehousing establishments convert to automated inventory systems, stock clerks need to be trained to use the new equipment. Stock clerks who bring merchandise to the sales floor and stock shelves and sales racks need little training.

Advancement

Stock clerks with ability and determination have a good chance of being promoted to jobs with greater responsibility. In small firms, stock clerks may advance to sales positions or become assistant buyers or purchasing agents. In large firms, stock clerks can advance to more responsible stock handling jobs, such as invoice clerk, stock control clerk, and procurement clerk.

Furthering one's education can lead to more opportunities for advancement. By studying at a technical or business school or taking home-study courses, stock clerks can prove to their employer that they have the intelligence and ambition to take on more important tasks. More advanced positions, such as warehouse manager and purchasing agent, are usually given to experienced people who have post-high school education.

Earnings

Beginning stock clerks usually earn the minimum wage or slightly more. Experienced stock clerks can earn anywhere from $5 to $10 per hour, with time-and-a-half pay for overtime. Average earnings vary depending on the type of industry and geographic location. Stock clerks working in the retail trade generally earn wages in the middle range. In transportation, utilities, and wholesale businesses, earnings usually are higher; in finance, insurance, real estate, and other types of office services, earnings generally are lower. Those working for large companies or national chains may receive excellent benefits. After one year of employment, some stock clerks are offered one to two weeks of paid vacation each year, as well as health and medical insurance and a retirement plan.

Work Environment

Stock clerks usually work in relatively clean, comfortable areas. Working conditions vary considerably, however, depending on the industry and type of merchandise being handled. For example, stock clerks who handle refrigerated goods must spend some time in cold storage rooms, while those who handle construction materials, such as bricks and lumber, occasionally work outside in harsh weather. Most stock clerk jobs involve much standing, bending, walking, stretching, lifting, and carrying. Some workers may be required to operate machinery to lift and move stock.

Because stock clerks are employed in so many different types of industries, the amount of hours worked every week depends on the type of employer. Usually stock clerks in retail stores work a five-day, 40-hour week, while those in industry work 44 hours, or five and one half days, a week. Many others are able to find part-time work. Overtime is common, especially when large shipments arrive or during peak times such as holiday seasons.

Outlook

Although the volume of inventory transactions is expected to increase significantly, employment for stock clerks is expected to grow more slowly than the average for all occupations through 2008. This is a result of increased automation and other productivity improvements that enable clerks to handle more stock. Manufacturing and wholesale trade industries are making the greatest use of automation. In addition to computerized inventory control systems, firms in these industries are expected to rely more on sophisticated conveyor belts, automatic high stackers to store and retrieve goods, and automatic guided vehicles that are battery-powered and driverless. Sales floor stock clerks probably will be less affected by automation as most of their work is done on the sales floor, where it is difficult to locate or operate complicated machinery.

Because this occupation employs a large number of workers, many job openings will occur each year to replace stock clerks who transfer to other jobs and leave the labor force. Stock clerk jobs tend to be entry-level positions, so many vacancies will be created by normal career progression to other occupations.

For More Information

For materials on educational programs in the retail industry, contact:

National Retail Federation
325 7th Street, NW, Suite 1000
Washington, DC 20004
Tel: 202-783-7971
Web: http://www.nrf.com

Supermarket Managers

School Subjects
- Business
- English
- Mathematics

Personal Skills
- Communication/ideas
- Leadership/management

Work Environment
- Primarily indoors
- Primarily one location

Minimum Education Level
- High school diploma

Salary Range
- $30,000 to $50,000 to $100,000+

Certification or Licensing
- None available

Outlook
- About as fast as the average

Overview

Supermarket managers work in grocery stores. They manage budgets, arrange schedules, oversee human resources, lead customer service, and manage each aspect of the day-to-day business of bringing the nation's food supply to the people. According to the Food Marketing Institute, there are 126,000 stores that sell groceries across the country and often several managers at each location.

Managers include store managers, assistant store managers, courtesy booth/service desk managers, customer service managers, receiving managers, and managers of such departments as bakery, deli/food service, food court, front end, grocery, meat/seafood, frozen foods, pharmacy, and produce/floral. The size and location of the store determines how many of these management levels exist in each store. In a small, family-owned grocery, the manager and owner may be the same person.

History

The supermarket industry, in the early 1900s, was really a group of small "mom and pop" grocery stores. At most of these stores, the owners or someone in their family managed the daily operations. The typical city street of that time resembled the supermarket departments of today with each store handling its own specialty. For example, the fish market and the bakery each had an individual owner and operator.

By 1902, Kroger, now the country's largest grocer, already had 40 stores and a factory as well as a management staff to keep the growing business efficient. As Americans began purchasing more of their food and relying less on their gardens and farms, the supermarket industry grew along with the need for professionals to manage the stores.

Technological innovations have increased the duties and responsibilities of supermarket managers. Bar codes, inventory systems, and complex delivery systems have increased the need for professionals who can use these tools to run an efficient store while still remembering that customer service is of utmost importance. With profit margins low and competition high in this $346.1 billion industry, careful business planning is imperative for each store's success.

At the beginning of the century, locally owned groceries were the norm, although some chains were already growing. However, that has changed with the rapid growth of chain supermarkets. While chains have purchased some local stores and companies, other small stores have simply gone out of business. The total number of grocery stores dropped from 150,000 in 1987 to 126,000 in 1999, according to the Food Marketing Institute.

Advances in technology will continue to alter the duties of the supermarket manager. Online grocery shopping, though in its infancy, is predicted to grow rapidly over the next few years. Qualified managers trained in the newest technology and management practices will be needed in this evolving industry.

The Job

Supermarket managers oversee a wide range of resources, both personal and professional, to do their jobs effectively. Their days are fast-paced and interesting; routine duties are often interspersed with the need to solve problems quickly and effectively. Steve Edens is the associate manager of a Kroger supermarket in Columbus, Indiana. Like most supermarket managers, Edens works a variety of shifts and handles a range of responsibilities. Working as the liaison between the corporate office and his staff, Edens spends time each day handling correspondence, email, and verbal and written reports.

Supermarket managers often work on more than one task at once. Edens carries a note pad and a scan gun, and pushes a cart, as he checks the floor, inventory, and departments each day. While checking the inventory, Edens uses the scan gun to check on an item that is low in stock. The scan gun lets him know if the item has been ordered. "The technology keeps getting better and better," says Edens. The average supermarket carries 30,000 different items so the technology of today helps managers to keep those items on the shelves.

You may think that managers rarely get their hands dirty, but this is not the case for Edens and other managers. He carries a feather duster with him as he makes his daily rounds of the store. Appearance is key for a supermarket's image as well as customer comfort, so Edens occasionally straightens and dusts as he surveys the placement of advertising material, merchandise, and other store features. The typical supermarket covers 39,260 feet, so managers must be prepared to spend a lot of time each day walking.

Planning is key for supermarket managers. They must prepare weekly schedules, which are carefully coordinated with the wage budget. The managers work with the head cashier to check and coordinate schedules. The manager and associate manager oversee an immediate staff of department heads that vary with the size and location of the store.

These department and subdepartment managers are in charge of specific areas of the store, such as the bakery and deli, frozen foods, or produce. The department managers, along with the store managers, interview prospective employees while the store managers do the actual hiring and firing of personnel. Large supermarkets may employ more than 250 people, so supermarket managers need to have good human resources training.

Department heads also handle specific promotions within their areas as well as customer service within those areas. Many store managers have previously worked as a department manager.

Promotion and advertising are also on the managers' list of responsibilities. "We always plan a week ahead on displays and sales," says Edens, noting that seasonal displays are important in the grocery industry as in any other retail industry.

One of the major responsibilities of each of the managers is customer service. Managers need to courteously and competently address the requests and complaints of store customers. "I like working with people," says Edens. "It's very satisfying to me when I can help a customer out."

Though Edens acknowledges that the compensation—both monetarily and personally—is high, he has worked many 60- to 70-hour weeks and most holidays. Many stores are open 24 hours a day, seven days a week, 365 days a year. With at least two managers required to be on duty at a time, supermarket managers can expect to work late nights, weekends, and holidays. "I don't think I've ever had a three-day weekend off," says Edens. "You work most holidays."

At larger stores, like the Columbus Kroger, scheduling is often easier and requires less hours from each manager since the load can be split up between a larger management staff. Managers at smaller stores should expect to work more hours, weekends, and holidays.

Frequent transfers are also common. Edens has worked at over 10 stores during his 24-year career. Though his transfers have not involved household moves, larger companies do pay moving expenses for management transfers.

Problem solving and quick thinking are key skills to being a successful supermarket manager. Delayed deliveries, snowstorms, or holidays can throw a wrench into schedules, inventory, and effective customer service. Managers need to deal with these problems as they happen while still preparing for the next day, week, and month.

Requirements

High School

Speech classes will help you build your communication skills, while business and mathematics courses will give you a good background for preparing budgets. Because reading is integral in evaluating reports and communicating with others, English classes are a must for workers in this field. Any specific classes in marketing, advertising, or statistics will also be helpful. Learning how to work well with others is important, so any classes that involve group projects or participation will help you to develop team skills.

Postsecondary Training

While a college degree is not required for a career in supermarket management, there is a trend toward hiring new managers straight out of college. Even for college-educated managers, stores have their own specific training programs, which may involve classes, on-site learning, and rotational training in different departments.

Some colleges offer degrees in retail management, but many people choose to major in business management to prepare for a management career. Even an associate's degree in retail or business management will give you an advantage over other applicants who only have a high school diploma.

Other Requirements

Interacting with people and handling customer service is the biggest requirement of the job. According to the Food Marketing Institute, the average consumer makes 2.2 trips per week to the grocery store. With this many people in each store, serving those people with professionalism and courtesy should be the number one goal of supermarket managers. "You have to be a people person to do this job," says Edens.

Supermarket managers should be able to handle a fast-paced and challenging work environment, and have the ability to calmly solve unexpected and frequent problems. Besides being able to "think on their feet," supermarket managers should be able to evaluate analytical problems with budgets, schedules, and promotions.

Exploring

If you are interested in becoming a supermarket manager, get a job at a supermarket. Any job, from bagger to cashier, will help you understand the industry better. Supermarket jobs are readily available to students, and the opportunity for on-the-job experience is great.

Interview managers to discuss the things they like and do not like about their jobs. Ask them how they got started and what influenced them to choose this career. When you set up your interview be sensitive to seasonal and weather concerns. Supermarket managers are extremely busy during holidays or other times when people flock to the stores in droves.

Look ahead. Online shopping is just one of the new trends in supermarkets. Be aware of new changes, and evaluate how your skills might fit into this changing industry.

Take some business classes. If you love people, but can't create a budget, this is not the career for you.

Hang out at your local store. Go on a busy day and a slow one. Study what activities are taking place and how management's role changes from day to day. Get a feel for the pace to decide if you would want to spend a lot of hours in a retail atmosphere.

Employers

Kroger is the largest supermarket chain and employer, operating over 1,220 food and convenience stores in the United States. Albertson's and Safeway round out the top three chains.

There are 126,000 stores that sell groceries in the United States. Over the past 10 years, the number of chain supermarkets has grown while the number of small, independent grocers has decreased. While this makes the number of stores and employers smaller, the larger stores need a variety of management professionals for a diverse number of positions, from department managers to store managers.

Grocery stores are located in nearly every city. Though smaller cities and towns may have only one or two supermarkets to choose from, in larger cities, consumers and prospective employees have a wide selection of chains and smaller stores.

Starting Out

You won't be able to start out as a supermarket manager; some experience is usually necessary before assuming a management role. You can start as a bagger or cashier or as a management trainee. There are two basic career paths—either working through the ranks or being hired after completing a college program. Edens started in the stock room and has worked in a variety of positions from cashier to department manager and now as an associate manager. Working in many areas of the store is an important part of becoming an effective manager.

"This is one of the few companies where you can start as a bag boy and become the president," says Edens. Hard work and dedication are rewarded so paying your dues is important in this career.

To be considered for a management position, grocery experience is necessary. Even other retail experience is not enough to be hired as a manager because the grocery industry has so many specific challenges that are unique to the field.

Cold call applications are readily accepted at customer service counters in most grocery stores, and larger grocers do on-campus recruiting to attract future managers. Newspaper advertisements are also used to recruit new workers for this field.

Advancement

Department managers can advance up the management ladder to store manager or associate store manager. After reaching that level, the next step in advancement is to the corporate level—becoming a unit, district, or regional manager, responsible for a number of stores. The next step at the corporate level is to vice president or director of store operations. Managers at the store level can advance and receive higher salaries by transferring to larger and higher-earning stores. Some relocations may require a move to another city, state, or region, while others simply require a bit longer or shorter commute.

Earnings

Supermarket managers are well compensated. According to the 1998 Food Marketing Institute survey, starting managers can expect to make $30,000 a year. Department managers at large stores average $50,000 annually. Store managers average $75,000, while district managers earn average salaries of $100,000 annually. These salary numbers may include bonuses which are standard in the industry. Pay is affected by management level, the size of the store, and the location.

Benefits are also good, with most major employers offering health insurance, vacation pay, and sick pay. While some supermarket workers are covered by a union, managers are not required to pay union dues and do not receive overtime pay.

Work Environment

Supermarkets are clean and brightly lit. Depending on the time of day, they may be noisy or quiet, crowded or empty. Nearly all supermarket work takes place indoors, and most managers will spend several hours on their feet walking through the store while also spending time at an office desk.

A team environment pervades the supermarket, and managers are the head of that team. They must work well independently while supervising and communicating with others.

Supermarket managers are expected to work more than 40-hour weeks and also work holidays, weekends, and late hours. Because many supermarkets are open 24 hours a day, rotating schedules are usually required. Also, calls at home and last-minute schedule changes are to be expected.

Outlook

Though the outlook for all retail managers is expected to be slower than average, managers in the supermarket industry should expect growth that is about as fast as the average. The number of stores is decreasing, but specialization and demand are growing in the industry.

"There is a big demand for qualified people," says Edens. "Supermarkets need people with experience, good records, and good people skills."

The growth in grocery management is due to an expanding line of inventory and specialization. Because there is strong competition in the supermarket industry, stores are creating new departments, such as restaurants, coffee shops, and video departments, to meet consumers' needs.

With total supermarket sales of $346.1 billion, the industry is huge and continues to grow as consumers spend more money on greater varieties of food and other merchandise. There will be a strong demand for people who can manage others while mastering the latest technology. Grocery stores are often at the forefront in exploring new technologies to improve efficiency, so computer literacy and business acumen will be increasingly important.

For More Information

For industry and employment information, contact:

Food Marketing Institute
655 15th Street, NW
Washington, DC 20005
Tel: 202-452-8444
Email: fmi@fmi.org
Web: http://www.fmi.org

For information on all retail fields, contact:

National Retail Federation
325 7th Street, NW, Suite 1000
Washington, DC 20004
Tel: 202-783-7971
Web: http://www.nrf.com

For information on mass retail careers and a list of colleges with retail programs, contact:

International Mass Retail Association
1700 North Moore Street, Suite 2250
Arlington, VA 22209
Tel: 703-841-2300
Web: http://www.imra.org/

Supermarket Workers

Overview

Supermarket workers are a diverse group. Each supermarket worker is employed in one or more areas of a grocery store, from the checkout lane to the deli counter to the back stock room. There are 3.5 million people who work as employees of food stores, according to the U.S. Bureau of Labor Statistics. Supermarkets are located in cities and towns across the nation and include large chains and locally owned stores.

History

Grocery stores have existed in the United States since the 1800s. Those early stores did not carry a wide variety of merchandise and brands. Many specialized in one area such as bread, fish, or meat. Even these early stores needed workers to help run their businesses. At the time, the workers were less specialized; often, the same person who helped wrap the meat at a butcher shop might be found later in the day sweeping out the store.

In the early 1900s, small "mom and pop" stores opened. These stores were the beginning of the modern grocery industry. Soon, some of the stores expanded into chains and the role of the supermarket worker became even more important. With bigger stores, more merchandise, and more customers, more people were needed to work in the stores.

While technology has eliminated positions in other industries, the grocery industry has wisely utilized technology (like the bar code system) but has not seen a need to reduce staff. While the technology has made efficiency and customer service better, people are still needed to do most of the jobs in a grocery store. One technological change on the horizon is online grocery stores. This is a very new trend, but even this online ordering will involve order takers, delivery personnel, stock room personnel, inventory control, and more.

The Job

What is it like to be a supermarket worker? It really depends on who you ask. There are so many different types of work to do in a grocery that each job can be very different from the next.

One of the first positions most people think of in a grocery is the *cashier*. Cashiers are on the front lines for the store's customer service and order accuracy. Cashiers greet customers, scan merchandise, record coupons, present totals, take payments, and help to bag groceries. It is each cashier's responsibility to keep his or her work area clean and to ensure that their cash drawers balance at the end of their shift. If merchandise is incorrectly marked or damaged, the cashier calls the appropriate department to assist the customer.

Along with the cashiers, *clerks* help to bag the groceries, and, if necessary, help the customer transport the grocery bags to their vehicles. *Courtesy clerks*, sometimes called *bag boys* or *baggers*, also collect carts from the parking lots and help provide maintenance for those carts.

Stock personnel play an important behind-the-scenes role in supermarkets. They help unload trucks, inspect merchandise, stock shelves, and track inventory. If you visit a grocery late at night, you can see these workers busily preparing for the next day's customers.

One of the trends in the grocery industry is specialization. The supermarket industry is very competitive, so stores are adding more services and conveniences to attract and keep customers. Some of the specialized departments have historically been a part of grocery stores, such as bakeries and meat markets, while others, such as restaurants and baby-sitting services, are new.

Each area requires workers with specialized knowledge and training as well as experience in the grocery industry. Butchers, bakers, and deli workers are generally dedicated to their individual department in the store while other workers may "float" to the areas where they are needed.

Other supermarket workers are responsible for certain areas such as produce or dairy. While there is no preparation work involved such as there is in the bakery or deli departments, these workers regularly inspect merchandise, check expiration dates, and maintain displays.

Many supermarkets now include a restaurant or food court which require food preparers, servers, wait staff, and chefs.

Many larger chain supermarkets have a pharmacy on-site. *Pharmacists* fill prescriptions for customers, as well as offer counseling on both prescription and over-the-counter medications. *Pharmacy technicians* assist the pharmacist by filling prescriptions, taking inventory, and handling the cash register.

There are also many specialized support positions in supermarkets. *Store detectives* assist with security measures and loss prevention. *Human resource workers* handle personnel-related issues, such as recruiting and training, benefits administration, labor relations, and salary administration. These are very important members of the supermarket team since the average large grocery store employs 250 people. Supermarkets also require qualified accounting and finance workers, advertising workers, marketing workers, information technology professionals, and community and public relations professionals.

Supermarket workers report to either a department or store manager. They may have to attend weekly departmental meetings and must communicate well with their management. Because many supermarket workers deal directly with the customers, their managers depend on them to relay information about customer needs, wants, and dissatisfactions.

Many supermarket workers work part time. For workers with school, family, or other employment, hours are scheduled at the time workers are available, such as evenings and weekends. Since many grocery stores are open 24 hours a day, employees may work during the day or evening hours. Weekend hours are also important, and most grocery stores are open on holidays as well.

All of the different jobs of a supermarket worker have one very important thing in common—they are customer-driven. Grocery sales nationwide continue to climb, and customer service is highly important in the grocery business as in all retail businesses.

With that in mind, the primary responsibility of all supermarket workers is to serve the customer. Many secondary duties such as keeping work areas clean, collecting carts from the parking lot, and checking produce for freshness are also driven by this main priority.

Requirements

High School

Many workers in the supermarket industry are recent high school graduates or present high school students. There is a large turnover in the field as many workers move on to other career fields. A high school diploma is not required, but enrollment in a high school program is encouraged if you do not have your degree. In high school, you should take English, mathematics, business, and computer science classes to learn the basic skills to do most supermarket jobs.

Postsecondary Training

Postsecondary training is not required in the supermarket industry but may be encouraged for specific areas such as the bakery, or for management positions. Stores offer on-the-job training and value employees who are able to learn quickly while they work.

Certification or Licensing

To protect the public's health, bakers, deli workers, and butchers are required by law in most states to possess a health certificate and to be examined periodically. These examinations, usually given by the state board of health, make certain that the individual is free from communicable diseases and skin infections.

Other Requirements

The most important requirement for a supermarket worker is the ability to work with people. "With every job I've done here, I've had to help people out," says Nick Williams, who works as a stock boy, bag boy, and cashier at Foods Plus supermarket in Columbus, Indiana. Because workers are required to work with both the public and their own management, communication and customer service skills are important. Following directions as well as accuracy and honesty are also important qualities that supermarket workers should have to be successful.

Exploring

The best way to find out about what it's like to be a supermarket worker is to become one. Openings for high school students are usually available, and it's a great way to find out about the industry.

Take a class in a supermarket specialty you find interesting. If you think the bakery looks like fun, take a cake-decorating class and find out.

Help out with inventory. Many grocery and retail stores offer limited short-term employment (a day or two a week) for people who can help with inventory during key times of the year. This is a good opportunity to get your foot in the store without making a greater commitment.

Talk to your friends or even your parents. Chances are that at some time, they have worked in a grocery store. Find out what they liked and didn't like about the work. Another source for information is your local grocery store. Talk with the people there about their jobs.

Employers

There are 126,000 grocery stores in the United States, according to the Food Marketing Institute. This number has dropped from 10 years ago when the total number was 150,000. These grocery stores are located across the nation, in towns and cities. Some are part of a large chain such as Kroger. Kroger is the nation's largest grocer with over 2,200 stores in 31 states. Albertson's and Safeway round out the top three chains. Other stores are a part of smaller chains or are independently owned.

Workers will have more employment opportunities in cities and large towns where several stores are located. In smaller towns, only one or two stores may serve the area.

Starting Out

Williams got his first job in the supermarket in the same way as many others. He applied at the customer service office at the front of the store. Williams was looking for a part-time job with flexible hours and applied at several retail stores in his area.

Besides walk-in applications, groceries use newspaper ads and job drives to attract new employees. Because some of the jobs a supermarket worker may do require little education and pay a modest hourly rate, there are often openings as workers move on to other positions or career fields.

If you apply in person, you should be ready to fill out application materials at the office. Neat dress and good manners are important when applying in person.

Many of today's grocery managers started out as high school clerks or cashiers. It is possible to turn a part-time job into a full-time career. "There are a lot of opportunities to learn different jobs, if you want to," says Williams.

Advancement

The opportunities to advance within a supermarket are good if you are dedicated and hard-working. It is possible, with a lot of hard work and dedication, to advance to a more specialized and better-paying position.

Supermarkets rely heavily on experienced workers, so while a college education might be helpful, it is certainly not required to advance in the field. Relevant experience and hard work are just as beneficial to advancement.

Steve Edens, an associate manager at a Kroger store, started out in the stock room and says that the supermarket industry is one of the few fields where you can start as a bagger and end up being the company president.

Earnings

According to the U.S. Bureau of Labor Statistics, the average nonsupervisory food store employee makes $9.05 per hour. Some employees may make less per hour down to the current minimum wage of $5.15 per hour, while more specialized workers in departments may earn more. In areas such as the bakery, workers may make more per hour while stock clerks make less.

Many supermarket workers are part-time employees and do not receive fringe benefits; full-time employees often receive medical benefits and vacation time. Supermarket workers often are eligible for discounts at the stores in which they work, depending on their company policy. The United Food & Commercial Workers International Union represents many supermarket workers concerning pay, benefits, and working condition issues.

Work Environment

Grocery stores are open 24 hours a day, so workers are required for a variety of shifts. Many supermarket workers are part-time employees and work a varied schedule that changes each week. Depending on the time of day they work, the store may be bustling or quiet. Most of the work is indoors although some outdoor work may be required to delivery groceries, collect carts, and maintain outside displays. Schedules are usually prepared weekly and most will include weekend work.

Supermarket workers work in shifts and must work with the managers and other workers in a supervisory environment. These managers may be within their department or within the entire store. They must follow directions and report to those managers when required.

Outlook

Though the number of grocery stores has declined in recent years, the employment outlook for supermarket workers is good. The field has a large turnover with workers leaving to pursue other careers. Many part-time employees are seasonal and must be replaced often.

As supermarkets add more conveniences for customers, workers will be needed to staff those areas. For example, adding restaurants to supermarkets creates a need for a whole new set of food service workers.

Also, although there are fewer grocery stores, consumers are spending more on groceries. According to a study by the *Progressive Grocer*, as reported by the Food Marketing Institute, consumers spent $449 billion on groceries in 1999. Ten years earlier, that figure was $313 billion.

One reason for the decline in the actual number of grocery stores is the trend toward supermarket chains. Many small chains and local groceries have been purchased by larger chains, and others have gone out of business in the face of the competition.

For More Information

For industry and employment information, contact:

Food Marketing Institute
655 15th Street, NW
Washington, DC 20005
Tel: 202-452-8444
Email: fmi@fmi.org
Web: http://www.fmi.org

For information about the retail industry, contact:

National Retail Federation
325 7th Street, NW, Suite 1000
Washington, DC 20004
Tel: 202-783-7971
Web: http://www.nrf.com

For information about working in retail, contact:

International Mass Retail Association
1700 North Moore Street, Suite 2250
Arlington, VA 22209
Tel: 703-841-2300
Web: http://www.imra.org/

Wireless Sales Workers

Business **Speech**	School Subjects
Communication/ideas	Personal Skills
Primarily indoors **One location with some travel**	Work Environment
High school diploma	Minimum Education Level
$35,000 to $68,000 to $110,000	Salary Range
None available	Certification or Licensing
Much faster than the average	Outlook

Overview

Wireless sales workers, also known as *cellular salespersons*, work for wireless telecommunications service providers to sell wireless products and services to individuals and businesses. The products and services they sell may include cellular phones, cellular phone service, pagers, paging service, and various wireless service options. *Inside salespersons* work onsite at their employers' sales offices, helping customers who come in to inquire about wireless service. *Outside sales workers* travel to call on various potential customers at their offices.

History

Although you may think of cellular phones as being a product of the late 20th century technology, they actually have their beginnings all the way back in the late 1800s. In 1895, an Italian electrical engineer and inventor named Guglielmo Marconi figured out how to transmit signals from one place to another using electromagnetic waves, creating the first radio. One of Marconi's first major successes came in 1896, when he was able to send signals over a distance of more than a mile. Marconi continued to improve and refine his invention. In 1897, he transmitted signals from shore to a ship at sea 18 miles away, and in 1901, he sent signals a distance of 200 miles. By 1905, many ships were regularly using Marconi's radio to communicate with the shore.

Radio evolved rapidly. By the mid-1920s, more than 1,400 radio stations were broadcasting programming all across America, and by the end of the 1940s, that number had grown to 2,020. Immediately following World War II, radio saw a period of especially rapid development and improvement. Sophisticated transmitting and receiving equipment played a key role in the exploration of space, and in 1969, astronauts on the Apollo mission used a very high-frequency radio communication system to transmit their voices from the moon back to earth for the first time.

Cellular radio, which is essentially today's cellular phone service, was first tested in the United States in the 1970s. This system, a miniature version of large radio networks, was named "cellular" because its broadcast area is divided into units called cells. Each cell was equipped with its own radio transmitter, with a range of about 1 to 2.5 miles. As a mobile "radiophone" moved through this network of cells, its calls were switched from one cell to another by a computerized system. It was only possible to make calls within the area covered by the network of cells, however; once the radiophone was outside the cellular area, the connection was lost. First tested in Chicago and the Washington, DC, area, this cellular system was soon duplicated in other towns, both large and small throughout the United States. As more and more of the United States became covered with these networks of cells, it became possible to use cellular phones in more places—and these phones became increasingly widespread.

In order to use a cellular phone, one had to have two things: the phone itself and a subscription to a cellular service. Cellular service providers, much like traditional phone companies, signed users up for phone service to be billed on a monthly basis. Often, as part of the sign-up agreement, the new customer received a free or inexpensive cellular phone. As the availability of cellular service has expanded geographically, the number of people signing up for this service has increased dramatically. By 1998, more than 55 million Americans were signed up for cellular service. Cellular, or wireless, sales workers in communities across the United States have been the liaison between the cellular providers and the cellular users. They have been the workers selling the service, explaining its workings, and signing up these new users.

The Job

Wireless sales workers sell communications systems, equipment, and services to both businesses and individuals. The products they sell may be divided up into "hard" products—such as pagers or cellular phones—and "soft" products, such as cellular phone service, paging service, voice mail, or phone service options. Most wireless sales workers work for a cellular service provider, trying to persuade prospective buyers to sign up for that provider's phone service. In areas that are covered by two or more cellular providers, the salesperson may have to convince customers to use his or her provider, instead of the competition. In other cases, it is merely a matter of convincing the customer that he or she needs cellular service, explaining what the service provides, and doing the paperwork to begin a contract.

There are two categories of wireless sales workers. Outside sales workers visit prospective clients at their offices. These workers may make appointments in advance, or they may drop in unannounced and ask for a few minutes of the prospective customer's time. This practice is called "cold calling." Outside sales workers often only call on customers within a specific geographic "territory" that may be defined by their employers. The second category, inside sales workers, work in a cellular provider's offices, frequently in a customer showroom. These workers greet and help customers who come into the office to buy or inquire about wireless services. Brian Quigley is the inside sales manager for a major cellular service provider in Bloomington, Indiana. Before becoming the manager, he worked as a sales representative for four years.

There are several aspects of a wireless sales representative's job. The first is generating new customers. Sales workers develop lists of possible customers in many different ways. They may ask for referrals from existing customers, call on new businesses or individuals as they move into their assigned territory, or compile names and numbers from business directories or phone books. They may also attend business trade shows or expositions, or join networking groups where they can make contact with people who might be interested in signing up for their service. Once sales workers have their list of possible contacts, they may send out letters or sales brochures, often following up with a phone call and a request for an appointment.

The second aspect of the job is perhaps the most important. This involves talking with prospective customers about the company's services and products and helping them choose the ones that they will be happy with. In order to do this, the sales worker must have a thorough knowledge of all the company's offerings and be able to explain how these offerings can meet the customer's needs. "We spend a lot of time each day taking sales calls from people or working with walk-ins," Quigley says. "And dealing with people who are considering buying wireless is not a quick process. On the average, you spend between 15 and 30 minutes with one customer, answering all of his or her questions." Answering these questions may involve demonstrating the features of different phones or pagers, going over the pricing structures of various service plans, or explaining how the wireless service works and what its geographic limitations are. The sales worker must try to overcome any objections the customer might have about the products or services, and convince him or her to make the purchase. If the salesperson fails to "close the deal" on the first visit, he or she might follow up with more visits, phone calls, or letters.

A wireless sales worker's job usually involves a certain amount of paperwork. When a salesperson makes a sale, he or she may input the customer's billing and credit information into a computer, in order to generate a contract, explain the contract to the customer, and ask him or her to sign it. He or she may also do the paperwork necessary to activate the new customer's phone or pager. Sales workers may also maintain records on all their customers, usually in a computer database.

Many sales workers maintain contact with their customers even after they have made a sale. The salesperson may make a follow-up call to ensure that the customer's service or product is working properly and that he or she is satisfied. He or she may also check back periodically to see if the customer is interested in purchasing "upgrades"—new or improved services or products. The sales reps in Quigley's location also help existing customers who have questions about their equipment, service, or billing statement. "You'd be surprised how much of my job is servicing existing customers," he says. "I'll bet I spend 80 percent of my time on customer retention."

Because wireless technology changes so rapidly, learning about new products and services is an important part of a wireless sales worker's job. He or she may frequently attend seminars or training programs to keep current on the latest in wireless products, in order to be able to explain them to potential customers. Quigley says that his company holds quarterly sales rallies, where wireless equipment manufacturers come to explain and demonstrate their new products. "A lot of the stuff you just have to learn on your own, too," he says. "Because things change so rapidly, you often can't wait until the next sales rally to find out about a piece of equipment. You just have to crack open the manual and read up on it."

Requirements

High School

The minimum educational level needed to become a wireless sales worker is a high school diploma. To prepare for a career in wireless sales, you should choose high school classes that will help you understand and communicate with people. Courses in speech, English, and psychology are all good options for this. You might also want to take classes that help you understand basic business principles, such as business and math courses. Finally, it may be helpful to take some fundamental computer classes, in order to become familiar with keyboarding and using some basic software applications. Like virtually all other offices, wireless offices are typically computerized—so you will probably need to be comfortable operating a computer.

Postsecondary Training

Although there are no formal requirements, it is becoming more and more common for wireless sales workers to have a two-year or four-year college degree. Quigley began his career in wireless sales after obtaining a bachelor's degree in marketing, and he says that his company prefers to recruit college graduates. Many employers consider a bachelor's degree in marketing, business, or telecommunications to be especially beneficial. In addition, because wireless services are so heavily dependent upon technology, some wireless sales workers enter the field with a technology-related degree.

Whether a new wireless sales worker has a college degree or not, there are likely to be aspects of the job and the company that he or she is not familiar with. Therefore, most wireless service companies provide training programs for their newly hired workers. These programs, which may last from three weeks to three months, cover such topics as cellular technologies, product lines, sales techniques, using the company's computer system, entering orders, and other company policies.

Other Requirements

Successful wireless sales workers have a combination of personal characteristics that allow them to do their jobs well. Perhaps the most important is the ability to connect and communicate with people; without these qualities, it is virtually impossible to be an effective salesperson. Wireless salespersons should enjoy interacting with people, feel comfortable talking with people they do not know, and be able to communicate clearly and persuasively. "You also have to be a good listener, in addition to a good talker," Quigley says. "When someone is upset, you have to hear what they are saying and be able to appease them." The ability to work in a high-pressure, competitive environment is also an important characteristic. Many wireless sales workers earn the majority of their income from commissions or bonuses. In addition, most workers are expected to meet monthly or quarterly sales goals that are set by the company. Successful sales workers should be able to handle the stress of working to meet these goals. Self-confidence is another essential quality of good sales workers. Any sales job will involve a certain amount of rejection from customers who are not interested or not ready to buy. Salespersons must be secure and confident enough to avoid letting this rejection affect them on a personal level. According to Quigley, the willingness to learn and change is also highly important to success in this field. "This industry is always changing, sometimes so quickly that it's hard to keep up with it," he says. "You have to be prepared for the changes."

Exploring

You can find out what it is like to be a wireless sales worker by visiting the offices of a local cellular provider. By talking with the sales staff and perhaps observing them as they work, you should be able to get a feel for what the day-to-day job entails. One of the best ways to find out firsthand if you enjoy selling is to find a summer or after-school job in sales. To learn more about wireless technology and the products available, visit your local library and see what books and magazine articles are available—or do some online research, if you have access to the Internet.

Employers

Most of the major telecommunications companies throughout the United States offer cellular service in addition to their traditional phone service. AT&T, Sprint, MCI, GTE, Ameritech, Bell Atlantic, Bell South, SBC Communications, and U.S. West all have wireless divisions—and, consequently, wireless sales staff. There are also many smaller wireless providers, such as United States Cellular, Nextel Communications, General Wireless,

Telecom, Paging Network, and others. Each of these smaller providers also has a sales staff, although in many cases a much smaller one. These providers are located all throughout the United States, in virtually every medium-sized and large community. You should be able to find a list of them by asking your local librarian for help or by doing a keyword search on "wireless service providers" on the Internet.

Starting Out

To find a job in wireless sales, you should first determine which wireless service providers operate in your area. Check directly with these providers to find out if they have any openings, or send them a resume and cover letter. If you are willing to relocate, you might contact the national headquarters of each of the large wireless companies mentioned above to find out what jobs are available nationwide. Many of these companies even have Web sites that list current job openings. You might also keep an eye on local or regional newspapers. Telecommunication companies, including wireless providers, frequently post job openings in the classified sections of these newspapers. If you have attended a college or university, check with your school's placement office to see if it has any contacts with wireless service providers.

Many wireless providers prefer to hire applicants with proven sales records. This may be especially true in cases where the applicant has only a high school degree. If you find that you are having difficulty obtaining a position in wireless sales, you might consider first taking another sales job—perhaps in electronic or communications equipment—to gain experience. Once you have proven your abilities, you may have better luck being hired for a wireless sales position.

Advancement

For most wireless salespersons, advancement comes in the form of increased income via commissions and bonuses. A proven sales worker might earn the title of senior sales representative or senior account executive. These workers may be given better territories or larger, more important accounts to handle. Some sales workers eventually move into managerial roles, as they expand in their capabilities and knowledge of the company. A sales worker might move into the position of sales manager, for example. In this position, he or she would oversee other salespersons, either for the entire organization or for a specific geographic territory. Quigley became the sales manager for his location after four years of working as a sales representative. The next step on the career ladder for him is general manager of retail stores, which would put him in charge of a specific geographic region. Another advancement possibility in larger companies is that of trainer. In the role of *sales trainer*, a sales worker would be responsible for developing, coordinating, and training new employees in sales techniques.

Earnings

For motivated and skilled salespersons, the pay for wireless sales can be quite good. Most companies offer their sales staff a small base salary, and incentive pay in the form of commissions, a bonus, or both. In some cases, the incentive pay can increase the salesperson's base salary by up to 75 percent. Because most salespersons earn the majority of their income through incentive pay, the income level depends greatly upon individual performance.

According to the 1998 *U.S. News & World Report*'s "Best Jobs for the Future," the average beginning wireless sales worker might expect to earn around $35,000. A senior sales worker might earn around $68,000, and a top sales executive could make as much as $110,000. Wireless sales managers could expect to earn between $75,000 and $80,000.

Sales workers who are employed by most wireless companies receive a benefits package, which typically includes paid vacation, sick days, and holidays, and health insurance. Outside sales workers may be provided with a company car and an expense account to pay for food, lodging, and travel expenses incurred while traveling on company business.

Work Environment

Inside sales representatives typically work in comfortable, attractively decorated customer showrooms. They usually have desks either in the showroom, or in a back office, where they can do their paperwork and perhaps meet with customers. While many sales reps work regular 40-hour weeks, Monday through Friday, it is not at all uncommon for these workers to work longer-than-average weeks. In addition, many wireless sales offices are open on weekends to accommodate customers who cannot come in during the week. Therefore, some sales workers spend weekend hours at the office.

Outside sales workers may spend much of their time traveling to meet onsite with various potential customers. Unless a salesperson's territory is very large, however, overnight travel is uncommon. When not traveling, outside sales workers may spend time in the office, setting up appointments with customers, keeping records, and completing paperwork. Both types of sales workers spend the majority of their time dealing with people. In addition to customer contact, these salespersons often work cooperatively with service technicians and customer service staff.

Outlook

Job opportunities for wireless sales workers are expected to grow much faster than the average for all other occupations through 2008. The number of people signed up for cellular service rose by 11 million between 1996 and 1998—a 20 percent increase. The sales of pagers and paging service also grew during this time. These numbers are expected to continue to increase. Part of the reason for this growth is that technological advances are making cellular phones and pagers more effective and useful all the time. One of the most recent developments, a microwave-based digital communication technology, is especially expected to increase wireless phone use by offering better quality and range. Wireless service is also being increasingly used to transmit data as well as voice. Examples of wireless data communication include such applications as faxing and Internet access. In addition, new technology and widespread use of cellular services have driven the prices of cellular service down, making it an option for many people who previously couldn't afford it. All of these factors combined should spur the need for a growing number of wireless sales workers. The demand for jobs will also be enhanced by the high turnover in the sales field as a whole. Each year, many sales workers—in both the wireless and other industries—realize that they cannot earn enough money or that they are not well-suited to the career, and leave their jobs. New sales workers must then be hired to replace the ones who left the field.

For More Information

For job postings, links to wireless industry recruiters, industry news, and training information, contact or visit the Web site of:

Cellular Telecommunications Industry Association
1250 Connecticut Avenue, NW, Suite 200
Washington, DC 20036
Tel: 202-785-0081
Web: http://www.wow-com.com

For the latest on the wireless industry, job information, and information about Wireless Magazine, contact or visit the Web site of:

Wireless Industry Association
9746 Tappenbeck Drive
Houston, TX 77055
Tel: 800-624-6918
Web: http://wirelessdealers.com

For information on the wireless industry in Canada, contact or visit the Web site of:

Canadian Wireless
500-275 Slater Street
Ottawa, ON K1P 5H9 Canada
Tel: 613-233-4888
Email: tvora@cwta.ca
Web: http://www.cwta.ca

Index